D. J. BLACKMORE

ISBN 978-0-646-97091-2
Cover: Alissa Dinallo www.alissadinallo.com
Copyright © 2017 by D. J. Blackmore
All rights reserved

Folly

To Dad
For buying me books
And Mum for reading them to me
For the firstborn
With faith hope and love enough to
Watch my steps
And for the children
Who have filled my arms
X

Acknowledgments

Sarahanne Miranda Field, BPsch (Hons) Msc. You've made a habit of being awesome. Even before the lives of Emma and Tobias, you've been beside me in a way that few can understand the language of. Thank you for listening, for speaking my tongue.

To the traditional storytellers of this land, I stumbled into the beauty of your dreamtime. I hope others may see some of it through my eyes.

And to my husband, Australian dirt bike racer Paul Caslick, great grandson to the nation's first indigenous rights activist, Charles Frederick Maynard of the Wonnarua:

> *'Your people shall become my people.'*
> Ruth 1:16

Prologue

The Colony of Newcastle New South Wales, 1822.

Frost paled the grass in the paddock. Dawn had already begun to break when the shovel hit the dormant earth. Light spilled over the river and over his progress as he dug. Birds opened chorus, a hallelujah to the day, but there was no glory in the unholy act, no blessing of the unsanctified rite. There were no mourners at the grave, save the birds in the treetops looking on. Summer had come and gone with the youth of the man in the shallow grave but winter's chill had kept him young, for the cadaver appeared almost fresh faced. The shovel was set down. The soil was dug away with curious hands.

The body had been here after all, just as he had hoped. Why he had done it, he had no idea. It was a flashback of the murderous moment that had reminded him of it. So he had come to see for himself, and he had been correct.

He perched on haunches, studying the face, smiling in this knowledge that was also his secret. Yet as the sun rose above the river and rested on the face of the dead, he hardly cared that anyone might find him hunkered down in the broad field. This pleasure was all his own, and it gave him great satisfaction.

One

It would not fit. The dress was too small. If the past two weeks had seen Phoebe eat more cake than was seemly, it was all too obvious.

The parson would be waiting. The bridegroom – doubtless pacing with stiffly starched collar – would soon begin to worry that his bride would not turn up. A flush swept up Phoebe's cheeks, but no matter however deeply she breathed in to minimise her waistline, they still weren't able to fasten the gown. Phoebe looked at Emma in dismay.

Emma's Aunt Adelaide lost all composure. She threw up her arms. Phoebe winced. 'Stop moving, Phoebe! Leave go of the seams or you'll tear the fabric!'

'But it is strong brocade, Mama.'

'The way you're pulling at it with those sweaty fingers, you'll tear the stitching, regardless of how sturdy the cloth may be.'

'What's to be done, Mama?' Phoebe's chin trembled.

'Why, we'll have to unpick it, child.'

'It will take too long!'

'Will wailing fix these bursting seams? Never! Now strip off, and we'll set to.' But the gown was stuck fast. It could neither be pulled down, nor up.

Aunt Adelaide wrung her hands. 'Oh, Phoebe, I fear there's no pulling you out. We shall unpick the thing where you stand.'

'But I must be at the church by the O'clock!'

'Then we need to be about our business, because you won't be at the church unless we can fasten your gown.'

Emma tried to soothe her cousin. 'Have no fear. We will have you to the church.'

With scissors and determination, Emma helped Aunt

Adelaide free her cousin Phoebe from her confines. Pins and needles were employed at a rate that Emma would never have thought possible, as they widened the girth of the gown that it might fit Phoebe as it had done only weeks before.

Tears rolled from Phoebe's lashes to run down her cheeks. 'I will be late.'

'And should have been at the church ere now, but your young man will wait, never fear.' Phoebe's mother's tone was brusque.

'You may wipe away those tears, for it is Emma and I who have suffered the pricks of these many pins. Still, all is done now. Let's not forget the veil to cover those tears, though for sure the congregation will think they are for joy alone.'

They looked up to the sound of the cottage gate being opened. 'Whoever is that knocking?' Aunt Adelaide frowned.

The door was opened by the help. The girl was just about to let the bridegroom in. Emma's Aunt Adelaide threw her arms up in alarm.

'Please do not let Mr. Ferguson in the door! Young girls are not permitted to see their beaux on the morning they are to take wedding vows, when tradition says that it's bad luck. Not that I believe in any such nonsense, but still ... '

'Oh, here now is the shopkeeper. An inopportune time, Mr. Tucker, but come in for just a moment if you've a mind to. Only, make sure Mr. Ferguson stays outside.' Aunt Adelaide peered around the shopkeeper towards the bridegroom, Rory Ferguson.

'Seems young men are ever keen to flout convention. Mr. Ferguson your bride will see you directly.'

Rory caught Emma's eye. He wore worry like a crumpled hat. Emma hoped her smile reassured him, but kept her counsel as Aunt Adelaide continued to vent aloud at impetuous love.

'I cannot think what is so urgent that it cannot be said after the church ceremony.' The shopkeeper said nothing, and her aunt continued. 'I had hoped that our eldest daughter Euphemie would find a young man in view of marriage. Goodness knows the girl is not the easiest of companions to live with. Now that her sister Phoebe is to be wed – and Euphemie without even a suitor – why Euphemie will be incorrigible, to say the least. She's not even here to help ready her sister to leave for church! I do not know what Phoebe and I would have done without our niece, Emma, truly I don't. She is a niece without parallel.'

Mr. Tucker stood patiently until her aunt had finished. He opened his mouth to speak.

He was too slow. Aunt Adelaide beat him to it. 'What brings you here, Mr. Tucker?'

'It's about the tea, ma'am.'

'Only please tell me that you have the order of China tea to take up to the rectory hall? I cannot for the life of me understand how either the parson's wife or myself could have forgotten to check with you. A jug of rainwater will quench the thirst, but will do nothing to still the nerves.'

A cup of tea was probably what her aunt needed right then, if only they could spare the time. Emma hoped for Mr. Tucker's sake that he had the China tea on request, for Aunt Adelaide was in no mood for nonsense.

Euphemie came to Emma's mind and she frowned. She hadn't seen her cousin since last night. Surely her cousin hadn't flounced off in jealousy because it was not her wedding day?

✠

Mr. Tucker thought the doctor's wife needed to calm down, but would never tell the woman so. He was small. The physician's wife was portly, ham fisted, and the widower had been married for enough years to know not to back-chat a woman in a stew.

'The tea is delivered already madam. One pound of tea to the rectory hall door.'

'But is it China tea, Mr. Tucker? We must have China tea. I do not like that inferior stuff from Ceylon. I don't give a fig what anyone says; it just isn't of the same quality.'

'No indeed madam,' he agreed, although truth to tell, he couldn't distinguish one from another. Tea was tea as far as he was concerned.

'Another thing, Mr. Tucker, and it is quite simply this: you allowed my daughter Euphemie to buy scarlet ribbons.' Mr. Tucker blinked.

'Do you not think, Mr. Tucker, that a young woman looks decidedly like a strumpet in scarlet?'

Thomas Tucker felt his Adam's apple bob up and down like a fishing float. If he so much as swallowed, the woman would have him hooked. She tried to bait him with her words.

'Can't you see that it makes a young woman look as though she is asking for attention?' He considered the right words to say. He had none.

'I always liked scarlet,' he told her limply.

She rolled her eyes. Appeared to think he was a dunderhead. 'So does every man, Mr. Tucker, and that's the whole problem.'

Mr. Tucker ventured a question. 'If the young lady isn't spoken for, what does it signify if she has a fancy to wear red ribbons in her hair?'

A hand went to her head as though it was all too much. Thomas Tucker flinched.

'The next time you sell ribbons to lasses with a penchant for scarlet, perhaps think to offer them ivory instead. It's far more seemly.'

Thomas Tucker took it as his cue to leave.

Pulling his hat down upon his head, he questioned whether

it would be wise to stock scarlet again. The ladies in the colony had taken umbrage over the fact that he kept little more than calico, twill and worsted. Well, if the women folk weren't content in that, from now on they could shop in Sydney. If it was more than kerosene, millet brooms or saltpetre that they wanted, they could buy their wares elsewhere. Because he would simply stick to what he knew best, and it wasn't women, of this he was certain.

It was no business of his if the girl wanted fancy ribbons. It wasn't his duty to safeguard or sermonise to would-be wanton maids. He was just a shopkeeper.

Two

Aunt Adelaide watched as the shopkeeper hurried down the road. A glimpse of the groom Rory Ferguson still lingering by the gate caught her attention.

Aunt Adelaide shook her finger at him. 'If you've changed your mind, Mr. Ferguson, it's too late!'

'Nothing could be further from my mind. I only wonder where your daughter is. It's after nine and Phoebe's not shown up.'

Emma's aunt frowned at the red haired young man through the window, seemed to recollect that the young redcoat was not supposed to be there. She shooed at him as though he was a sand fly come lately off the beach.

'Go back up to the church, young man. We will meet you there directly.'

'But she's a full half hour late!'

'A bride is supposed to be late, and will be later still if you don't leave our door! How will she get past with you mooching for her attention?'

Aunt Adelaide glanced back to see her daughter Phoebe standing by the bedroom door. One warning look from her mother was enough. Phoebe dutifully disappeared.

Aunt Adelaide's voice rose. 'If the groom leaves the church, why the whole congregation will think the wedding's called off!' Her words had the desired effect.

Aunt Adelaide flinched as the cottage gate slammed shut and Rory Ferguson jogged hurriedly back up the road.

'Where on earth is Euphemie? I haven't seen the chit since supper last night. I don't know whether to be incensed with the girl for trying to ruin her sister's special day, or worried for her whereabouts. If she is making herself scarce out of jealous spite,

I shall be disappointed indeed.'

'Don't let it spoil this wonderful morning for you.'

'I shan't,' she vowed, with a determined pull of her skirts, as though she would gain the obedience of the fabric, if not her disobedient daughter.

Phoebe stood in the doorway. 'I haven't seen Euphemie either, Mama.'

'She is doubtless already at the church. And so my dear should you, if you've a mind to wed that Irishman.'

Was Euphemie there waiting with the congregation? Emma only hoped that it was so. A flag of unease rose within her. Surely there was nothing untoward regarding the absence of her cousin?

✠

The first person Adelaide saw as she entered the church was Mr. Freeman. A coarse sort of a fellow. He was polite enough, Adelaide supposed, but he was still indentured to the crown, whether he had been given his freedom or not.

Still, the young man was a better choice for her husband's niece Emma than Gideon Quinn had ever been. When she thought about how close Emma had come to marrying Gideon, Adelaide could hardly believe that she had instigated the match between her niece and that scoundrel. For too long he had baited Adelaide, but no more. Gideon Quinn had had his comeuppance. If revenge was a dish best served cold, then she had partaken full and well.

Adelaide wiped her brow and looked around for Euphemie. Nowhere in sight. She spied the parson's wife and sat down.

'Tobias is quite the gentleman,' Mrs. Brown nodded. 'Why, he could be mistaken for the groom, so handsome he is!'

Irritation bunched like a tight chemise. 'I hadn't noticed. Still, he cuts a well enough figure I suppose. Yet he hasn't always been as his name suggests, Mrs. Brown, and we both know it. I would never allow Mr. Freeman to consider himself suitable for either of my daughters, Euphemie or Phoebe.' Adelaide's smile was grudging. 'He's only just recently been allowed to hold his head up with the dignity of a free settler. The groom may well be an Irishman too, but he's a lieutenant, not an emancipated convict.'

How the woman championed the man! Need the parson's wife talk of Mr. Freeman right now?

'Your Phoebe looks a picture. You must be so proud of her.' Adelaide nodded and smoothed the ruffled skirt of her gown.

'I thought Euphemie would wed before Phoebe, and yet here the girl doesn't even want to turn up to her sister's wedding.'

Mrs. Brown looked shocked. 'Where is she?'

Adelaide's hands were restless in her lap. 'I don't know.'

Mrs. Brown whispered, 'Whatever keeps the girl I wonder?'

'All I know is that the chit is trying my patience sorely. I don't know whether to be worried over her absence, or just plain angry.'

The parson's wife nodded and squeezed Adelaide's hand in a gesture that was meant to comfort.

A thought struck Adelaide. The commandant had set off only this morning for Sydney. Surely Euphemie would never follow the man? Adelaide was of the notion that where the commandant was concerned, Euphemie forgot dignity altogether.

She wondered where she had gone wrong in mothering that girl. How could two sisters be so unlike in every way? Adelaide looked up as a feather from her headdress drifted to the floor. She followed its descent with her eyes, then realised that Parson Brown was speaking.

Adelaide was brought back to the moment. Noiselessly she repeated vows along with Phoebe. The years had begun to dim her eyesight, but they had yet to steal the memories of her own special day so many years ago.

White petals were strewn as a carpet for the bride and groom. Handfuls of blossom were bright as scattered clouds. Phoebe and Rory Ferguson had entered the church as two people, and had emerged from the church as one. She tried to swallow her emotions but it was no use. She wiped her eyes.

Even as cups of tea were shared in celebration of her daughter's marriage, Adelaide still watched for Euphemie.

It had been an eventful morning and she was jarred by the clink of teacups and silverware as the hot brew was stirred. Laughter was louder than the lorikeets that screeched from nearby trees, and Adelaide put a hand to her head.

This vicar's wife whispered loudly, 'I haven't seen Miss Euphemie anywhere.' Was the girl no more than a scrap of paper misplaced under the furniture, blown by the wind, unobserved by the eye? Adelaide tried to ignore the woman.

Knowing her friend well, Adelaide guessed that Mrs. Brown wanted to try and cheer her, but the morning had worn her patience threadbare.

But Mrs. Brown would not cease. 'Wherever has she gone?' Adelaide ground her teeth, and wished her silence would still the woman's tongue. Mrs. Brown poured two cups of tea. The spoon jingled above her voice as she wondered aloud,

'You must be vexed?' Then, when she got no response, 'China tea does wonders for the nerves, I always think. A cup is just what the doctor ordered,' and because Adelaide was the doctor's wife, Mrs. Brown tittered at the joke.

The raucous birds left the trees overhead in a flurry of noise and colour. Adelaide put her hands over her ears as they took flight, but not before she felt her temper snap.

'I cannot agree with you on that, Mrs. Brown. I am inclined to think that this China tea is very inferior stuff indeed, because I can hardly bring myself to drink one drop!'

THREE

The elderly woman surveyed the shore. With monocle poised in her hand at the ready, the crone's eye lit on the colony. Wigged and powdered, she was more like a spectre of the eighteenth century come to life, than an elderly lady of the present day.

A boy at Emma's left exclaimed, 'Oh look its Judy from the puppet show.' He was given a sharp word and a quick clout. The sharp hooked nose, the savage eye; the looking glass brought down upon the side of the ship with an impatient hand like some tiny hammer on a side street stage.

She glanced down at the youngster who still watched '*Judy*'. He lifted his arms and legs as though he too was a marionette. 'Are you Punch?'

'Aye,' He flashed a grin then brought a small fist down upon his head a few times and acted as though he saw stars.

'Have you been naughty, Mr. Punch?' He smiled as Emma joined in on his act.

But the boy's mother turned on him; 'If you cannot behave Tom, you will not come with me to the wharf next time a ship sails in.'

Tom was brought to a halt. His arms flopped to his sides, red face painting his embarrassment. A ship sailing into port was always a curiosity for the whole colony, yet perhaps even more so for a young boy with dreams leagues wide.

Aunt Adelaide was fascinated by the old woman too. She stood, open mouthed, and whispered what sounded like a curse.

'I would never have thought to see her this side of the grave.'

'Who is she?' Emma asked.

Aunt Adelaide turned to face Emma. 'She, my dear, is known as Trouble.'

'Trouble' came all too soon.

With eyeglass in one hand, cane in the other, the powdered crone made toward the edge of the brig, as though the clogs she tottered on would overbalance her. Two sailors went to her aid. She swiped at them with her cane. They dodged, but weren't quick enough, and although the blows were ill-aimed, they were menacing enough. Both sailors made a retreat and the old woman scowled. The walking stick pointed a finger of malice.

'Lay those hands upon me again, and it will be once too often!'

'She is oldest lady I've ever seen, Ma,' Tom said.

Aunt Adelaide began to hurry away. 'I just don't know why she isn't dead.'

Emma blinked, following her aunt's retreat. The woman's tone was full and running over with venom.

The old woman called from the boat, holding up the monocle again as she was lowered to the water in a row boat. 'Violet? Violet, is that you?'

Aunt Adelaide reeled back. Her neck and face were flushed purple.

'Yes, it is! It is,' the old woman assured herself. She turned to the captain of the ship, 'I'd know the strumpet anywhere!'

Emma's hand flew to her mouth.

'I believe, madam, that the lady is wife to the surgeon.' The captain's reply was loud enough to reassure everyone on the dock.

'I don't care who she's married to, my good man. She is who she is ... twice the size that's true, but I'd know her anywhere, so I would.'

Oh, how sound carried across the water ...

Emma followed on her aunt's heels as the woman puffed up Prospect Hill. It was possibly the fastest she had walked in years. She blew like a bellows as her bosom heaved. It wasn't until they reached the lip of Prospect Hill that her aunt turned to scan the wharf.

'Heaven help me,' it sounded heartfelt enough. Emma followed the line of Aunt Adelaide's vision.

The curmudgeon had allowed herself to be helped from the row boat, and it appeared that she was still looking their way.

Aunt Adelaide moaned. 'Come, Emma. Let's take ourselves home.'

There was comfort in the cottage as Aunt Adelaide shut the door. Smells of salt beef, bread and homeliness. Aunt Adelaide stood in the parlour. She stared into the distance but didn't share her thoughts.

'Who is she?'

Adelaide turned to Emma. 'All in good time, Emma dear, but for the moment, a cup of tea?'

Emma quietly set about taking out the teacups. Her aunt had come to depend on her since Phoebe had left the nest.

Since Euphemie had run away.

As Emma tasted the China tea her aunt had been so eager to buy from Mr. Tucker for Phoebe's wedding, she thought about Euphemie, and wondered where on earth her cousin had gone. Had she followed the commandant to throw herself at him, as Aunt Adelaide bitterly supposed?

A brief investigation had revealed nothing, and because the commandant had sailed to Sydney town to conduct business on behalf of His Majesty, no one was able to ask if he harboured a female stowaway until he returned.

Uncle George urged, 'Come, Adelaide my dear. We'll ramble down to the shore. It will clear your head. Exercise is not only just good for the legs. It is good for the soul, too. Look at me: few would be able to tell that I had ever fallen beneath the cart.'

His duties at the hospice might have been curtailed, but

they had not stopped his cheerful determination.

'I may not be the head surgeon anymore, and have so many less patients I am responsible for, but will you allow me at least to be responsible for you?' He indulged Aunt Adelaide with a smile. 'Besides, the fresh air will do us both good. Heaven knows we have enough trouble on our plates. It sits heavy, I know. I say we walk some of it off.'

'What if the harridan's there?'

'Then we meet trouble head on.' He took her hand. A gesture of gentle strength that often comforted her aunt.

But it was not so this day.

'What if she talks, George? What if she tells the colony what I was before you drew me away and saved me from all that? I thought bad luck had died with Gideon Quinn. I hardly thought that the woman who had born him would come to continue where her son had left off.'

The woman was the mother of Gideon?

'All of us have made wrong choices at one time or another. No one is perfect. No one is without blemish. Anyone who is a true friend will disregard the idle chatter, because they know you for the good woman you are. They will forgive you.'

'As you forgave me.'

Emma turned away to busy herself. It was no business of hers whether Gideon's mother had decided to pay the colony of Newcastle a visit, and still less to question Aunt Adelaide's past.

Four

They had only just sat down to supper when there was a knock at the door. Emma intercepted a look between her aunt and uncle. Emma went to answer it. She anticipated Tobias's return even though she knew it couldn't be him. He had business in Sydney.

Gideon Quinn's mother stood at the threshold. Roughly rouged, less than five feet tall, her mouth brash the moment she opened it.

'Is the madam at home?'

The turn of phrase reminded Emma of some questionable epithet for women of ill repute.

'If you will wait a moment, I'll find out.'

Emma's assurance fell on deaf ears, because the old woman called in at the open door, 'Violet! Violet are you at home?'

'Perhaps you have the wrong address? There is no person by the name of Violet who lives here.'

'Not any more, there isn't.'

Emma turned. Aunt Adelaide stood staunch as a bulkhead.

Her name was Violet?

'It's all right Emma. I will attend to this.' Her aunt patted Emma's arm, yet her tone was brusque. Her aunt would brook no quarrel from the woman at the door. She addressed the elderly visitor. 'Cecily, it's been many years since I called myself Violet.'

The woman waved it away. 'I've come to see my son.' Aunt Adelaide didn't dispute it.

'I regret to be the one to tell you, Cecily but your son Gideon is dead.' Aunt Adelaide didn't sound regretful at all.

Understandable to anyone who had known Gideon Quinn.

If Emma expected Cecily Quinn to collapse in a crumpled pile of striped sateen, then she was surprised. Gideon's mother pointed a finger in the direction of Aunt Adelaide.

'I don't believe you! I have sailed thousands of miles to spend my last days with my son and you think I am going to believe that you don't know his whereabouts?' The elderly woman began to cough. She bent double, leaning against her cane.

Uncle George took the visitor by the arm and led her to a chair until the coughing stopped. Then, as Emma watched, Cecily Quinn took a pipe from her pocket and proceeded to pack, light and puff on it until her spluttering turned to a comforted wheeze.

'Wretched thing, can't live with it, can't live without it.'

Emma's uncle frowned and pushed his glasses further up the bridge of his nose.

'You would do well without it, to my way of thinking, madam. Sometimes a little of what you like does not always do you good.'

'I have come to the ends of the earth to see my only child, and you tell me he is dead? My health is the last thing on my mind.' Water sprang to her eyes and spilled down her cheeks. She blinked through her tears, when her eye alighted on someone to blame.

'So tell me, Violet, tell me what happened to my son. Now, I have all the time in the world, and I'm not going anywhere until you do.'

But the explanation was Emma's duty alone to give. She took a deep breath, choosing the right words before she stepped forward.

'Gideon and I were going to be married.' It was a tentative beginning. An introduction of sorts. Cecily Quinn turned her gaze towards Emma.

'What did you say, girl?'

'Gideon was my fiancé.'

'And I'm the wife of King George the fourth!'

Uncle George said, 'What Emma tells you is true.'

Cecily narrowed her eyes, surveying Emma. She felt the stare of appraisal. Yet it hardly mattered any more if she met the expectations of Cecily Quinn or not.

'Where does my son lay?'

'He rests at the new settlement of Wallis Plains.'

'I want to be taken to the cemetery there.' Cecily stood, as though the matter was settled. As though Wallis Plains was a mere walk away.

'He is in no graveyard.'

Gideon's mother fairly shrieked. 'What? Why doesn't my son lay in consecrated ground?'

'He is buried beside what was to be our new home on the banks of the river.' The woman grappled with the idea – at a loss for words – if only for a moment.

'Who can take me there?'

'I can.'

Emma spun to see Tobias entering the cottage. Again her heart tripped, this time for gladness.

'I worked on Quinn's Folly. I've been given an unconditional pardon, and slave for no man, but I'm willing to be your guide.'

'*Quinn's Folly?*' Cecily demanded 'And who are you, my man, that you can slight my dead son – a soldier of the crown – and yet are nothing but a convict, I'd like to know?' Cecily rose from the chair, chin thrust out. Her eyes flashed in her powdered face. She swiped at her tears with the back of her hand.

Tobias gave a slight bow. He flushed and glanced at Emma, who felt the slight for what it was.

'I didn't know that Gideon Quinn was your son, and it's sorry I am whenever a mother loses a child. I'm a government man no longer but if you can but pardon my past, I'll take you to

Wallis Plains before the week is out.'

'That's not good enough; I want to go there now, this minute. Take me to the wharf.'

Uncle George spoke up. 'As Tobias just explained, he is a convict no more. If you want to go to Wallis Plains sooner than he has offered – and graciously at that – then you will need to make other arrangements.'

'And where shall I stay in the meantime, I want to know?'

'That isn't our concern, Cecily. We have troubles of our own without borrowing anyone else's.' Aunt Adelaide turned away then, as though to signal the end of the engagement. Her aunt's lack of cordiality was understandable, the woman's long journey and grievous disappointment aside.

'I board at an establishment in the next street,' Tobias suggested. 'There may be a bed for you there.'

Cecily appeared grudging. She looked Tobias up and down. But she did condescend to nod.

'Take me there.'

His brows rose as he met Emma's eye.

Cecily pulled aside the striped skirt as she negotiated the door-frame, then stood at the cottage gate looking back, her cheeks stark.

Face powder couldn't putty her grief.

Tobias stood close to Emma for just a moment. 'I'll be back directly.'

A ghost from the past had just sailed out of the room, and though Aunt Adelaide sighed in relief, the fact remained that Euphemie had still not returned. There were not many places in the colony that a young woman could go without notice. Did Tobias have anything to tell concerning her cousin? Would Euphemie follow Commandant Morisset to Sydney, with or without his permission? It was a question they all wanted to know, but none more so than her aunt and uncle.

'I wonder whether Euphemie will soon be home.' Had Aunt Adelaide read her thoughts?

'I would not be at all surprised. Doubtless Tobias will have some information for us.'

But Uncle George's cheerful attempt fell without remark. Emma wished that her unapproachable cousin would walk through the door with the sea breeze. Euphemie would never be like her sister, sweet Phoebe, but she was her parents' daughter all the same, and they loved her as though the sun rose in her eyes.

'I will go and ask the commandant if needs be,' Aunt Adelaide vowed. 'I am flummoxed to know where that daughter of ours can have got to, George, and I just don't know what to think.'

Tears ran down Aunt Adelaide's cheeks. She put her head in her hands. Uncle George stood by stoically. He clasped her shoulder in gentle support, looking out towards the street for an answer, for a voice; for Euphemie.

'It is Sunday tomorrow, and we can both speak to Commandant Morisset after the service. He's an upright man my dear, and I am sure if our daughter did make a nuisance of herself, then he rebuffed her efforts as any gentleman would.'

Adelaide threw up her hands. 'The chit was jealous of Emma. She thought her cousin was competition, and here Emma was fond of Tobias all the while. Instead of throwing herself at the commandant, she should have waited for him to show interest in her.'

'Euphemie has always had a mind of her own.' Uncle George said it fondly. They all turned their heads at the sound of voices. It was the newlyweds: Phoebe and her husband Rory, and with them came Tobias. Emma's smile of welcome was for the man she loved.

'Where is Euphemie?' Phoebe looked around.

'We don't know,' her mother told her, palms outstretched.

Phoebe misunderstood.

'Did she say she was going somewhere?'

'I can't remember the last words we spoke to one another, Phoebe,' her mother continued. 'I haven't seen her since the night before the wedding. And if she had plans to up and leave us, then she didn't think to tell me.'

'She can't be far away?' There was a note of disbelief in Phoebe's voice.

'We thought,' Phoebe's father began, 'we wondered if perhaps she had stowed away on the brig the commandant had sailed on. We had hoped that it was not the case, but now your mother and I only pray that it is.'

Tobias spoke quietly. 'I never saw her.'

Emma read the apology on Tobias's face. Aunt Adelaide gasped, but Phoebe was still trying to understand the situation.

'Why would Euphemie have sailed to Sydney with the commandant anyway?'

'Did you not know that your sister had her sights set on Commandant Morisset?' Aunt Adelaide's words were mournful. There was an unutterable sadness in her smile.

'So you think that she stowed away and waited in his cabin? Is that what you're suggesting?' Phoebe was incredulous.

'Sure and don't you think Toby here would have noticed if she had?' Rory ventured.

Uncle George spoke. 'There is only one person to ask.' They all considered him for some moments. Then Tobias and Rory nodded in unspoken intent, and both men left the cottage with a mind to find out the truth.

In the distance the bells of the colony pealed, as they did so often during the course of each day. But today the sound was ominous in the cottage, and as her uncle placed a log of wood on the fire, Emma realised that she was still chilled in the little house.

Aunt Adelaide began to cry again in the stillness of the four walls. The sound was broken only by the logs as they burned and shifted in the fire, and further away still, the hush of waves as they reached the shore. No one spoke as they waited for the two young men who'd gone out into the sunless afternoon.

'*I never saw her*,' Tobias had said. But perhaps the commandant had.

He was the first to appear at the doorway, followed by Tobias. But it was Tobias's eyes that spoke without saying yet a word. Her gaze flickered to the commandant, and to Rory, yet she already knew.

'I can tell you nothing. I only wish that I could,' the commandant said. 'It's true that she waylaid me the other evening.' He looked down at his boots and re-framed his words. 'Your daughter bid me good evening Friday past as I was walking back to my quarters from my usual Friday evening card game. I assume she was taking the air. It wasn't the first time I had seen Miss Euphemie walking out as I returned home on a Friday evening.'

'Are you suggesting that she went out to meet you on your way back to the barracks?' Aunt Adelaide stood up. Uncle George put a steadying hand on his wife's shoulder. She shook off his touch.

'I had wondered whether this was so, madam, but I asked no questions and should make no assumptions.'

'Is it possible that our daughter could have stowed herself away somewhere on the brig en route for Sydney? That she may have escaped notice?' Uncle George wondered.

The commandant was slow to speak, deliberating his words. 'I am more than happy to have the brig searched, and will do so directly.'

But he never answered the question asked of him.

Uncle George saw the commandant to the door.

Five

'It was cold in that church.' Kevin shivered, meeting Tobias in the paltry warmth outside. 'Miserable as sin we were, up in that gallery. If the government men were clothed in decent slops, I'd be a sight warmer.'

'An unconditional pardon means that I can afford to buy myself a jacket. But it doesn't sit well that there are those that go cold and hungry while I'm well fed,' Tobias apologised.

'I was a Peepin' Tom for long enough to know that I was going to get caught eventually, Toby lad. I wasn't hungry, just greedy, if you get my meaning.' Kevin said, 'I didn't steal to feed my family. I knew what I was about. I've long since acquainted myself with the truth. There was a time I would have loved to blame anyone else but me, but then I wouldn't have met and married Mary.' He grinned. 'And, Toby my lad, if you hadn't been convicted for the term of your natural life, you would never have met Miss Colchester. You would still be slogging day by day in old Ireland. Now you can hold up your head in society. You're a gentleman in your own right.'

'What about Allan Campbell? The young Scot that Quinn smote with a shovel?' Tobias asked.

Kevin shrugged. 'Parson says that the rain falls on the just and the unjust.'

'Must have rained hard on Allan Campbell that day.'

'Let it go, man,' Kevin's voice was soft as the mist that fell around them.

'Easier said than done. When I'm asleep, I have no control of where my fears take me.' Tobias sighed. 'As I sleep, I imagine I can hear Quinn once more, threatening to tell the commandant that it was me that killed Campbell, before I throw his lifeless body in the sod of that unhallowed ground.' Tobias turned back to Kevin and shook his head. 'And then in the next part of the dream, Quinn asks me who will give credence to a man once convicted of murder, when the lies of one of the king's men trips off the tongue so smooth? And I know he's right, the devil that he is, and it matters not one ounce that I'm innocent of the crime. God knows, Kevin, I'll remember that day for the rest of my life.'

'It's only a dream, Toby lad.'

'I know,' Tobias nodded. 'but it feels a bit better to be reminded of it.'

'It'll pass. Quinn can't harm anyone this side of hell. When you and Miss Colchester decide on marriage it's sure to set your mind at rest. And can you Adam and Eve it?' Kevin asked, slapping Tobias on the back.

'I would believe anything, Kevin, coming from you,' Tobias joked.

Kevin's partly toothless mouth was a rickety gate of congeniality. The man looked as though he was sixty if he was a day, but a lot of the men, women and children were missing quite a few of their teeth. Kevin was no exception, yet was spry, for all that.

'Mary is in the family way,' Kevin crowed. 'And can you guess who the daddy is?'

'Well, since she's your missus, I'm hoping you'll say it's you,' Tobias grinned.

'Some of my intelligence must have rubbed off on you when we were living together in that cottage. Before you became a man of means, that is.'

There was no sarcasm in the remark concerning Tobias having become a member of polite society, and Tobias knew that Kevin was pleased for his good fortune.

'Sure and who nobs it with the parson and his wife, I'd like to know? I can't remember being given all the perks you seem to get, when I was lucky enough to work for them.'

'I won't say no to the parson's nose when they happen to invite me, Mary and little Katy to the manse for Sunday chicken roast.'

'I bet you've never eaten a roast fowl in the whole of your life,' Tobias wagered.

'There's always a first time, Toby,' Kevin agreed. The two men laughed.

Tobias shook his friend's hand with sincere pleasure. 'Congratulations, Kevin, you'll make a grand da. Just like the fine job you do with Mary's little Katy.'

Dread came over Tobias as he recalled the disappearance of Emma's cousin. Here he was laughing with Kevin, when he ought to have been thinking of things far more pressing. He scanned the congregation. Groups drifted and chatted beneath the huge trees clustered around the church on Prospect Hill.

'The surgeon's eldest daughter Euphemie hasn't been seen since Friday last. They'd hoped that she'd stowed away with the commandant on his way to Sydney, but I was on that brig and I never saw her. They went over that brig with a fine-toothed comb, but found nothing. I cannot for the life of me think where she might be.'

'Why did you travel on the brig to Sydney, Toby? Was it for business or pleasure?'

Tobias looked down at his boots and grinned. 'You'll find out soon enough.'

'I'm surprised that the doctor and his wife are even here at all.'

Tobias shrugged. 'Perhaps they wanted company. Sitting alone in their cottage wouldn't help.'

The strain of missing their daughter Euphemie saw the

couple stoop-backed and hollow-eyed, waiting for news; hoping for the best, fearing the worst.

A dark shape caught the corner of his eye; Cecily Quinn. The winter wind pulled at her mourning skirts as it would a dark bird on the wing. She fixed a sharp eye on him and headed in his direction.

'Who is this coming towards you?'

'She is the mother of Gideon Quinn.' Tobias sighed. He had hoped to avoid her this day.

Kevin almost choked on his surprise.

'Well, then that's trouble I just don't need,' and without another word he was gone.

'I need to know which day we will leave to go to this place you call Wallis Plains,' Cecily Quinn began before even she had reached him. 'The proprietress of the boarding house would like to know how many days I will be gone, and if in fact I will return at all.'

'There are not many places to stay at Wallis Plains,' Tobias explained. 'It's only a new settlement and you may be a little disappointed. It's nothing in size compared to the colony here.'

'Did someone not tell me that my son was the owner of a newly built home?' Cecily asked.

'Yes, that's true,' and he could have reminded her that he had helped build the house, but he didn't. That he was once a convict wasn't exactly a source of pride. 'You might want to ask Emma if it is possible for you to stay there a time.'

'And why should I do that, young man?'

'Well, Emma was engaged to Officer Quinn,' he began, not sure he felt comfortable with where the conversation seemed to be heading.

'But they were not wed,' the woman reminded him, 'so that doesn't make her his next of kin. That would as a matter of fact be me.'

She threw him a cunning smile as though she had put down a trump card. As though they had both played the game and he'd lost.

Tobias looked at Cecily. He realised then that he had expected to make a life on the wealth of Quinn's Folly. Maybe the folly had been his alone.

Cecily acknowledged the disappointment in his face with a slight smile. His cheeks warmed with a disconcerting flush. He had been under the assumption that Emma was Quinn's sole heir.

It appeared he had been wrong.

The old woman looked at him, sharp knowing in her pallid eyes. She flaunted triumph with a canny smile. He had no right to be irritated by her good fortune, but he was annoyed nonetheless.

Six

Emma was attentive to the commandant even though she was aware of Tobias standing close by Cecily Quinn. It had been so many days since she had the leisure to speak with Tobias, and waited only for a chance. Yet Euphemie was still missing. Her uncle and aunt needed all the support she could give them, but more than that, they needed their daughter Euphemie to be found.

Her own needs would have to wait.

'A search party is going to step out the colony.' Commandant Morisset told her. 'I'm going to have a couple of the Awabakal natives join in. The black trackers know how to read the signs around them far better than anyone. I have assured your uncle that we will find Miss Euphemie, and I intend to do exactly that.'

'Thank you, Commandant Morisset.'

'The party will assemble first thing tomorrow morning. The colony still has to be run, but there are men I can spare.' He turned to greet the officer before him.

'Miss Colchester, please excuse me, I have an errand I must attend. But allow me to introduce you to Officer Octavius Gray.'

'How do you do, Miss Colchester?'

'Well, thank you, Officer Gray.'

'As well as can be expected, under the circumstances, one might say,' the officer concluded. Emma nodded at the truth of his words.

The officer turned his head at movement in the periphery of his vision. Emma smiled as Tobias approached. Octavius Gray, however, only frowned.

'What can I do for you, sir?' Gray's words were polite, but his tone was cool. He spoke to Tobias with the air of someone used to communicating with those beneath him. Obviously he saw Tobias as such a person.

'I'd like a word with Miss Colchester.'

Octavius Gray's brows rose. His countenance spoke displeasure. 'Are you acquainted with this gentleman, Miss Colchester?'

If it was his intention to snub Tobias, he most certainly succeeded. Tobias wore an ominous scowl. 'Miss Colchester and I are well acquainted.'

The officer's brows lifted. 'Then I will say good morning.' He graced Emma with a stiff bow before he walked away, not bothering to give Tobias even a cursory nod.

'I would have introduced you, but ... '

Tobias shrugged her words away irritably. 'If you did, do you think he would have lowered himself to shake my hand?' Emma looked away.

'Aye, you know the answer to that as well as I do.' Tobias sighed and sought to reassure her. 'I'm not cross at you Emma, it's just that I don't take kindly to an aristocratic upstart who believes that because he was born with a silver spoon in his mouth, he doesn't have to extend civility to anyone else. His manner towards you, now that was an entirely different thing.'

'Why is that, Tobias?'

Tobias raked back his hair with a look of frustration. 'Because you're a beautiful woman he has his eye on, because you're more in his class; and because you and I are leagues apart.'

'Not to my way of thinking we're not. It doesn't matter to me what he believes, Tobias. Nor anyone else, for that matter.'

Tobias scowled towards the direction Officer Gray had gone. Legs braced, arms folded.

There was anger in his stance and in his heart, and although the sting of the lash had gone, it still left scars and they were tender yet.

'It is not worth the fight, Tobias.'

'Aye, it is. It is worth the fight. You are worth the fight.'

Emma reached out. She reached out to reassure him. 'Then the fight is won, for I give myself freely.'

Seven

Kevin found his wife after the service. 'I'm just going to have a word with young Toby. You and Katy walk on ahead and I'll catch up.'

'Will you be home by tea time, do you think?' little Katy asked.

'Have you been listening to your ma's cheek? Are you suggesting, Katy girl, that I could talk under water with my mouth full of marbles?' Kevin pretended horror. Katy giggled.

'She knows it for Gospel,' Mary smiled.

'Hen-pecked as bad as a baldy rooster, that's what I am!' Kevin cried, whipping off his hat to show Katy his thinning hair. Katy laughed, covering her mouth to stifle the sound.

And then Kevin said to Mary in hushed tones, 'I think they're going to conduct a search party for the surgeon's daughter.' Kevin glanced at Katy, who had trailed away, picking sprigs of grass and tiny flowers that lined the road.

'It'll be a sober Sunday lunch the surgeon and his family will be having,' Mary shook her head. 'The surgeon saved Katy's life. If it weren't for him, Katy would have died last summer. I hope they get their daughter back,' she whispered.

He shut out the possibilities and thought of the needs of his own growing family, nudging Mary gently in the direction of their cottage.

'Go and put your feet up, Mary love. I'll be home soon.'

Katy and her ma continued their walk. Katy had exhausted the small pickings in clear view, and cast her eye around for more further afield. Her ma waited as Katy stooped to pick them.

'There's a red one!' Katy pointed.

She skipped away and dropped to her haunches, only to realise that it was actually a ribbon, bright as the blood that had sprung out when she had stubbed her toe just days before.

She pulled at the ribbon, half buried in the dirt. To her delight, she was able to uproot it from the soil with a tug. It was followed by part of a mouse-brown plait that flicked up the dirt as she yanked at it in its bed.

It was long and thick as a hemp rope down by the wharf. Katy didn't want that, and couldn't have pulled it free even if she wanted to. Still, it was longer than her hair, and ... '

'Katy, let go of that at once!' Her mother was beside her and grabbed her hand to drag her back. She pulled her out of the scrub and away from the red ribbon in the soil. Ma had started to cry. Katy began to cry too.

'I'm not cross, Katy love,' ma told her, squeezing her hand tight. But Katy had never see her ma upset like this before. She squinted against the grey glare of the sky. A seagull wheeled overhead. Katy watched it high above her. It made a crying sound as it flew. Another sound caught her attention. It was the commandant walking down the road towards them. Katy's eyes were full of tears as a new fear struck her.

'Will the commandant be mad at me?'

'Of course he won't. He will thank you for finding ... for finding something that was lost.' Katy frowned a little. She had wanted that red ribbon, but if the commandant wanted it, she knew there would be no chance of getting it now, because the commandant told everyone what to do. Why did ma have to go and stop the commandant?

'Excuse me, Commandant Morisset!' she called out.

'Good day to you, madam,' the commandant said.

Katy wasn't going to give the commandant any kind of hello. But ma gave her a well-meaning poke. So she dipped a curtsy, but she didn't smile, and she hoped she looked as sour as that lady in black she had seen in church that morning.

All powdered up and pale as a ghost, the lady had mean eyes, and had fixed them on her as Katy had danced out of church.

She supposed she should have walked like a little lady as her ma often told her to do but she had been so happy to escape at the end of Parson Brown's sermon and the hard pew, that she hadn't thought to stop herself.

Her mother hadn't noticed, but the lady in black had. She had made some complaint to Parson Brown and he had just smiled and given the lady a sermon, as he always did, except not nearly as long. Something about little children getting blessed by Jesus, and how bad people weren't going to go to His kingdom if they were mean.

The old lady had made a noise that sounded like she had a frog in her throat. Katy had looked up at Parson Brown and he had given her one of his patient smiles, much like the commandant was giving her now.

Katy blinked and stopped scowling. She smiled and hoped it was like the parson's instead. It seemed to work, because the commandant gave her a humbug that he took from somewhere inside his coat.

Katy shoved it in her mouth.

'Katy, where are your manners? Say thank you to the commandant.'

'Thank you, commandant.' Katy sucked back on sweet juice and settled to look out at the harbour. When she was a grown-up, she would be able to see over the entire harbour.

'Commandant Morisset, there's something over in the scrub you might want to investigate.'

The commandant frowned. He looked in the direction pointed out to him and shrugged. He shook his head in puzzlement, looking back to Katy's mother.

'What kind of thing do you refer to? I see nothing untoward.'

'Neither did we until we went over closer to pick flowers.'

Katy looked up at her mother, who started to cry again. The commandant passed her a handkerchief.

How many other lovely things had he in the coat he wore? Maybe he found things and kept them, and when other people found things, they gave him those as well.

The commandant was like the king. Perhaps if she told him where his lost ribbon was, he might give her another humbug, because the one in her mouth wasn't going to last long.

She stopped her tongue moving and let the saliva puddle inside her mouth.

'Come and I'll show you,' Katy told him. The runny sugar dribbled from the corner of her mouth and she slurped it back. She tugged at the commandant's hand and made a valiant effort not to crunch the sweet between her greedy teeth and be done with it.

Ma told her to come away. She called from the roadside, but Katy had already bent down, pulling the commandant with her. She put out a hand to finger the scarlet bow. It was as bright as the commandant's jacket and she reached out her hand and grabbed it. The plait snaked after the ribbon. Then the commandant snatched Katy's hand away.

'Don't you want the ribbon?'

But the commandant didn't answer her. With a nod to her mother and scarcely a word, the commandant strode away. Katy looked up at her ma.

She was all pasty and swayed like the rigging on a ship. Then, bending double in the grass, her mother was sick.

Perhaps if the commandant had given ma a lolly too, it might have settled her stomach.

Peppermint juice welled in her mouth. Katy swallowed.

Katy stood there next to ma. There was the smell of vomit and the taste of peppermint. Katy looked back, and as her mother's back was turned Katy ran into to the scrub. She pulled the bit of satin. The bow unravelled. The ropey braid didn't want to let it go, but with one more yank, the ribbon was hers. The ground cracked as the ribbon gave way. Katy held it tight in her grubby hand and trotted back to her mother. The commandant hadn't wanted it. Katy did. Now the ribbon was hers.

Katy wanted to get home and find a safe place for her treasure. She dragged at ma's hand, skipping along. When they arrived at the cottage, Katy ran to the mattress on the floor. Her bed was pushed against the wall, and in the crack between her pallet and the wattle and daub wall, she got down and hid it.

Eight

Aware that Aunt Adelaide was uncomfortable that an emancipated convict dined at their table on the odd occasion, Emma had paused as she set out the supper crockery not so long ago.

Aunt Adelaide had said, 'Twenty-five dollars and an unconditional pardon doesn't change what he is, George.'

'What he is? What is he, pray tell? If Emma loves Tobias, then they have my blessing, and when her time of mourning has finished, I will be the first to offer him her hand.'

'What will people think?'

'I for one don't care what people think. It's so easy to judge a man without ever having walked his path.'

Emma had moved out of earshot then. Eavesdroppers never heard well of themselves. She was hurt for Tobias's sake, yet her aunt's point of view was one not so very different from many of the free settlers in the town.

Yet this morning Aunt Adelaide had surprised Emma when she had answered Kevin's good morning as he doffed his hat. Uncharacteristic behaviour when normally she would have disdained the convict, giving him a wide berth.

Uncle George supported his wife, as she leaned on his arm. He kept up a brave front, which was exactly that. As he smiled, offering a good morning to those who passed, Emma saw the bow of their shoulders, the unsteadiness of their gait. Everyone turned when the commandant and a party of officers proceeded down the road at a pace. There was something in the commandant's manner that was unsettling.

As the redcoats marched down the street, Kevin made himself scarce, probably to the security of his cottage. An indentured convict wasn't encouraged to mix with polite society, and the presence of the constabulary was enough to remind him of the fact.

Tobias turned to her. 'I must go with the commandant. You saw him beckon me?'

She nodded. 'What does he want, do you think?'

'I don't know.' Yet his face told more than his words.

'The commandant told me that the search party was tomorrow?' Emma glanced down the road at the backs of the retreating soldiers, and then back at him.

Tobias shrugged. 'I hardly like to guess.'

'Go. Lunch will wait. I'll set your plate aside.'

He gazed down at her for just a moment, and his look told her how much he loved her.

'Your uncle and aunt ... ' he began.

'I will tell them you'll come presently.'

Tobias squeezed her hand. With that small reassurance he left her, following smartly on the heels of the commandant.

Mist had rolled into the harbour. A grey blanket that silenced the day. With no sun to mark the passing hours, the atmosphere was strangely oppressive. Emma's aunt and uncle must have drifted away, so she made her way to their house. There was hardly a breeze to stir her skirts.

'Come and warm yourself Emma, dear.' Uncle George stepped away from the blaze so that she might stand closer. The fire gave off light and warmth if not cheer, and it seeped through the cloth of her gown and into her bones.

Aunt Adelaide sat on the high-backed settle with Phoebe, who got up and chafed Emma's hands.

'I don't know whose fingers are colder, Emma, yours or mine.'

'Top of the morning to you, Miss Colchester.' Rory Ferguson cleared his throat as though he would have liked to take back the jovial greeting, unfortunate sounding as it was.

He was as unaware as the others that the commandant had

just marched past on a duty no one would have expected this bleak winter Sunday.

'Now, the meat is hot, and the plates are warm, so let's give thanks and set to before all grows cold,' Uncle George pulled his waistcoat down over his stomach, as he was wont, and Emma noticed that it wasn't tight around his girth anymore. He had doubtless lost his appetite like the rest of them, poor Uncle George.

'I don't want anything.' Aunt Adelaide made no effort to leave the comfortable seat by the fire.

'Nonsense, Adelaide, doctor's orders,' Uncle George remonstrated. 'I'll carve the meat dear, and bring a plate over to where you sit. Heaven knows it's a dull day. Sit beside the fire and I'll be there with it presently.'

'Euphemie is missing and all you can think about is roast mutton?' Her aunt stood, quivering in anger and despair. 'I don't care if a mouthful of meat never passes my lips for as long as I live!' With that she left them, closing the bedroom door behind her with a bang.

Uncle George stood at the table, knife poised over the leg of mutton, his face the picture of defeat.

Phoebe's eyes were full of unshed tears. 'It's all right, Father,' Phoebe touched his hand. 'You've done nothing wrong.'

He met his daughter's look, and a tear fell from his cheek and onto the lamb. 'I do apologise.' He hastened to put down the carving knife and pulled a handkerchief out of his waistcoat pocket.

'You have nothing to excuse yourself for, Uncle George. This is a worrying time, and no one expects either you or Aunt Adelaide to be at your best. None of us are.'

He tried to smile and failed, beginning another subject instead. Anything, rather than dwell on the possibilities so close to home.

'There is cake too, my dears. Never fear that the maid has left us short of sweets.'

They were fortunate that they hadn't had to fully rely on their own resources since Euphemie had disappeared. But it was a solitary meal they ate, and the sweets lifted the spirits of no one.

Her uncle wondered, 'Where is Tobias?'

'He had to speak to the commandant.' Emma busied herself by arranging Tobias's plate. When she looked up, Rory Ferguson's look was quizzical.

The pendulum clock counted time as they ate their meal and the waves lapped the shore, and still Tobias did not return.

Nine

When Tobias reached the commandant, the men had already begun to scour the surrounding area.

'I was alerted to this not half an hour ago,' the commandant told Tobias. 'I'm afraid that there will be bad news for the surgeon and his family.'

'I feared as much. A young girl doesn't just go missing in a place like this. Outside the colony there's just miles and miles of bush.'

'I want you to identify the body, if you would be so good. I would have asked Ferguson, but my guess was that he was at the cottage of his wife's parents, and the last thing I wanted to do was alert them before I had to. I was acquainted with the young lady, but cold weather notwithstanding, the body will still be relatively decayed. To be on the safe side, you understand?' He waited for a response.

There was nothing else for it. Tobias nodded. It was an onerous task, but a necessary one. He would do what needed to be done.

Octavius Gray sauntered over. 'We can't find the ribbon, sir.'

'I saw it there myself only a short while ago. It must be there. If an infant can find it, I'm sure half a dozen grown men can.' Commandant Morisset seemed to recollect his manners, cleared his throat and began an introduction.

'Tobias Freeman, let me acquaint you with Officer Gray. Octavius, this is Tobias Freeman. He saved Miss Colchester from drowning, a child from being poisoned, and then to cap it off, apprehended a felon who had the authorities stumped for some time. I have to admit, I was a mite impressed myself.'

'I was expecting you to tell me that he can raise people from the dead as well.'

'Under the circumstances, that's a rather unfortunate quip,

Gray,' Commandant Morisset chastised the younger man. Gray had enough grace to look abashed. He glanced at Tobias then, and Tobias knew without ever a word being exchanged, that he and Octavius Gray would never see eye to eye.

'I can't for the life of me understand why they haven't yet found the ribbon.' The commandant's tone was irritable. He pulled at his collar and tweaked his cuffs, then after a few minutes, turned to point out the direction once more.

'What does the ribbon signify?' Gray wanted to know.

The commandant looked at the officer as though he was slow to understand. 'There is a plait on the other end of it. A little girl took me to where it was, and before I realised what it meant, she was twirling this rope of hair uncovered from the soil. I don't think the child had any idea what was on the other end of the plait. I hope she didn't at any rate.'

'Found it, sir!'

'No ribbon, commandant, but a long mousy braid!' another called out.

Tobias's innards gave a careless twist. The disturbance of his stomach above the waves, the sound of shovels against dirt and gravel. The eddy of his gut stirred the muddy sediment of his breakfast and water seeped into his mouth. He took a lungful of salt air. He would not vomit.

'Come, let us have this dark business done with,' the commandant said.

Tobias braced himself and followed the commandant wordlessly. The earth was damp from intermittent showers and the spades cut the earth with ease. The body was unearthed in minutes with minimum effort, so shallowly had the body been buried.

But it wasn't the sod that gave the skin that ruddy look, nor the damp that caused the skin to glisten surreally in the grey light. The eyes were not Euphemie's – at least not any more –

yet they were opened. Pale and blind, they stared out yet saw nothing. Dark specks flecked them, as though stars had burst into life in the moment of death.

'I will give them word.'

Commandant Morisset met his look and nodded. 'I would appreciate that.' But Tobias found himself rooted to the graveside, strangely unwilling to move, even as he contemplated the body.

It smelled like any other slightly ripened carcass. The body of a newly slaughtered lamb was little different. Only it had been someone's daughter, someone's child; one of the reasons they wanted to wake up every morning. Tobias passed a shaking hand over his face and braced himself with fresh air.

It wasn't only one life that had been cut short. There was a family in the cottage just up the road who would always wait for her to come back even though they knew she never would.

He wanted to strike something or someone. He kicked at the gravel. When Gray flippantly asked no one in particular, 'Was she only a convict then?'

Tobias shook his head. 'You know, I can't decide whether you're trying to make a holy show of yourself, or whether you're just plain stupid.'

'Say that again, sir and there will be more than one body to bury.'

Tobias ignored the commandant's pointed look. 'What difference does it make who or what she was? A life is a life. What does it matter whether she was high bred or low? She was a mother's child.' He shook with anger at the callousness of the man. 'Aye, I've come to the conclusion, and it hasn't taken long: you just aren't the full shilling.'

Octavius Gray put his hand upon the weapon at his side. Tobias spat the words. 'I prefer to fight like a man.'

'Gentlemen,' the commandant spoke up. 'This disagreement

has gone on long enough.'

'The man questions my intelligence ... my character!' Gray hissed.

'Aye, but more than that, I question your honour,' Tobias said. With a nod of good day to the commandant, Tobias strode off to deliver the news. As he went he heard Octavius Gray remonstrating with his senior officer, but the commandant wouldn't let him vent his spleen. Tobias glanced behind him and saw the commandant walk away.

It hadn't been hard to see how Euphemie's end had come. One plait was still wrapped around her neck, as though it was a post to tie a row boat. How was he to tell that to the surgeon and his wife? There was no easy way. He didn't care about his own discomfiture, only the pain it would cause a handful of people who had never asked for this kind of suffering. There was no best way to go about it.

In the end, he said very little.

The family looked up at his arrival, wide-eyed with both fear and hope.

'It is cold out there, Tobias,' the doctor told him. 'Come and take the chill off your hands. I believe Emma has some lunch put by for you.'

Tobias heard the man's words but there was only one thing on his mind, and food was the least of it. 'I'm very sorry to say they've found your daughter's body.'

He heard Euphemie's mother. She sent up a cry that went through the roof. She shook her head at his words as though she would deny the truth if she could. He watched Euphemie's father, who had fallen into a chair, head in hands. Then after long moments, he looked up, searching Tobias's face.

'How?' The surgeon pleaded, at a loss.

Emma's aunt had collapsed to the floor and was being

supported by Phoebe and Emma. Tobias went to the man and spoke quietly, so quietly that the women might not hear.

He looked into the doctor's eyes and saw understanding dawn, and with it a look of unspeakable pain. The man forced himself from the chair and knelt before his wife.

When Tobias turned to look at Phoebe's husband, he realised that the tears on Rory's cheeks mirrored the ones on his own.

Ten

The Worimi tribe kept to themselves. They had little trust in the whites. They used the native women and abused the native men, and if the blacks hoped to use the power of their women for barter, they were usually given short shrift.

The whites took without giving back anything in return. There was no love lost between the two cultures. When Lily found the redcoat amongst the reeds, she got nothing but scowling looks from the others.

Her uncle grunted. 'What d'ya want that white fella for? He's no good to us. You want his coat? Then take it off him, but leave him there.'

'They might wan' us to return the white fella.' Lily's smile was bright in her dark face. Her uncle made a non-committal sound, and prodded the soldier with his foot. The soldier didn't move. Water oozed from the jacket and over her uncle's toes as his foot made contact with the sodden man. He looked down, waiting for movement.

'Think he might've swallowed up too much water. He doesn't look like much,' her uncle considered.

'Do any of 'em?'

Her uncle grinned. 'You think they gonna give us anything back in return if you can heal him?'

Lily thought about it. 'He might.' She pointed at the redcoat. Her uncle shrugged.

The man in the red coat was no convict. He was one of the tribe of some big king who lived beyond the sea.

Yet her uncle frowned and scratched his head. The soldier's cheek was pulpy. It was swollen and the torn flesh of his face had flapped like the belly of a gutted fish as they had dragged him from the water. As Lily gingerly felt the man's skull she noticed a small wound, like a break in the bone of his head. Both her and her uncle knew enough about fire sticks by now to know that it was one of them that had done the damage.

'He's old,' her uncle told her. She nodded.

'He's ugly, too,' he concluded. 'If you want him, you get him, but I'm not gonna help.'

With grudging consent, and no effort promised on his own part, Lily's uncle left her to make up her own mind.

Lily hunkered down on her haunches, inspecting the 'ugly' soldier. Still, she hadn't seen any of them who could be called anything less. With their white skin and pale eyes, it made Lily feel as though she looked at the sky through the bones of the dead. Like skulls left to bleach on anthills, the light of a winter's day blinking through their eyes.

Lily pushed back the eyelid of the soldier with a curious thumb and forefinger to stare down at the unknowing man. Just as she had suspected, the eye was cold grey blue. The other one was blind and milky white. Lily shuddered and let go, wiping her hand on the grass.

Her uncle was probably right in everything he said. But Lily was curious. Could she heal the man? Maybe he would give the tribe some reward if she saved his life. Unwilling to touch such pale hands, Lily walked around the body and grabbed one booted foot. She tugged the unconscious man in her wake, pulling with all her might as she made for the home fire. The good smell of fish cooking in the coals at her people's camp, made her mouth water.

Her mother looked up as Lily approached. She eyed the scarlet coat as though the injured man could somehow curse her, spread disease that would wipe out the whole tribe, without so much as a glance.

'Whaddaya doin' with that white fella?' her mother demanded.

Lily spoke calmly. 'I thought I mighta be able to save him.'

Her mother looked at her in disbelief. 'Daughter, sometimes you as sharp as a gidya spear, why you actin' so stupid now?'

Lily shrugged. 'If someone saved me, I'd be thankful.'

Her mother made a noise in disgust. 'All they do is take, Lily. Haven't ya learned that yet?'

Maybe her mother was right, but she still wanted to mend him. Her grandmother had handed down her knowledge of healing, and Lily just wanted the chance to put it to some use.

There had been the bird that had fallen from the nest. She had tried to save it and had failed. Maybe this time she would succeed. Perhaps the white fella with the red coat would give her one of those lacy umbrellas she had seen the pale ladies hold above their heads like miniature humpies, keeping off the sun. But if he died, she would get to keep his coat at the very least.

Lily put out a timid hand to touch the bright buttons. They shone gold like the sun that came up over the water every morning. The scarlet wool was brighter than the breast of a king parrot, yet it was nothing like fur or feathers, or even hide. When the man's arm twitched, Lily jumped and fell back, landing on her seat. She scrambled back and left him where he lay, beside the warmth of the fire. It was time to collect the medicine she had learned about.

Between the rocks some onion lilies grew. Star-like yellow flowers stood up tall from the hollow spiked stems. Lily dug down deep and collected the bulbs for her mother on the way to gathering medicine. The corms were nice and fat, and when her mother threw them onto the coals, they would be sweet. The gift might even sweeten her mother's sour looks. One of the bulbs, though, Lily was going to crush and use as an healing wash for the soldier's face. Then she picked tea-tree leaves and eucalyptus, and wrapped it all in a sheet of paper bark.

When she came back, the redcoat was awake. He lay with his back to the fire, just as she had left him, but there was no mistaking the icy eye in the half-hollowed face, following her as she walked. At first she didn't even realise he was awake, or even yet alive. But then he blinked and Lily stopped, still as a heron.

He was aware of his surroundings, and of her, and a shiver ran up her spine at the sight of him. Her uncle had said he was ugly; all she knew was that he had looked more harmless asleep than he did now.

Her mother hissed, 'You should'n brought him here. The men were going to stick him with a spear. I wish they had, but one of the elders said if they did it might bring the tribe bad luck. If he dies, it's on ya own head, Lily, because you dunno what kind of curse his spirit will bring down on us. He should'a been left in the reeds to rot, away from here, away from our people. The elders and the other men, well, they angry.' Her mother spat into the dust, as though to rid her mouth of poison.

Lily swallowed hard, clutching the paper bark. Her excitement had gone, her stomach was hollow. Perhaps her mother was right?

She put the bulbs down in front of her mother who took them without a word and threw them on the hot ashes like a charm against evil. Lily knew without being told that her mother wouldn't be happy that the man be given even a mouthful of tucker.

In the coming days, Lily bathed his face and the wound in his scalp. She fed him as though he was one of them– though no one but her would go near him– and almost from the moment she had brought him into the camp, Lily wished she hadn't.

She told him many times what her name was, but he only ever called her

'*Gin*'.

Eleven

Tobias opened the door of his room in the boarding house and listened. There came the sound of clogs upon the stairs. The smell of tobacco smoke met his nostrils. A high powdered wig came into view, and then the forward jerk of her shoulders as the woman came towards him with a relentless cough. The last person he wanted to see and the only one in the colony he dreaded; Cecily Quinn.

He couldn't go down to breakfast in the dining room, but that the woman was there. In no corner of the establishment could he find peace. She would follow him with a gimlet look so sharp he could feel her eyes prick his spine. Now here she was before him again, with a new question, a fresh demand or more gossip.

'She wasn't always called Adelaide, you know,' she confided. 'When I was acquainted with her in London, she went by Violet.'

The landlady stopped to listen openly. Cecily's audience had increased to two. She saw the Scottish woman's interest and drew the landlady deeper into the conversation with a conspiratorial tone.

'Made more quid in one night than her surgeon husband probably makes in a week,' she winked.

'Really?' The landlady leaned in.

Tobias made to walk away without comment, but Cecily detained him with one bony hand.

'It's true,' she asserted.

'Aye, well it's no business of mine.' He was curt. Cecily narrowed her eyes, her neck gathering into her shoulders as if ready to strike. She tottered towards him on her clogs.

'I only mention it because of her rudeness. She could have put me up for the night, but she never even offered, and here's me having known her in London.'

The landlady shook her head. 'I had always thought her to be a good class of woman. It seems I was wrong about her. And you, you poor dear, slighted after traveling all these miles with such sad disappointment when you got here. Why, it makes me riled.'

Cecily snorted. 'She can hide behind her doctor husband, but she can't hide from me. Nor can she wipe out the past.'

'I'll not be listening to any more of this talk,' Tobias said. 'And let me ask you this, Mistress Quinn, how came you to know so much about a woman you're now wiping your shoes upon?'

He took in the powder, the pomade and rouged cheeks. 'A saying I've heard more than once is this: it takes one to know one. Now if you'll step aside, I'll bid you both good day.' Tobias pulled on his hat and strode out the door, before Cecily Quinn could peck him to pieces. Whatever the two outraged women wanted to say about him, they could doubtless do a better job without him being there.

He made his way past the cemetery, recalling the sadness of Euphemie's funeral the day before. Tobias shut the vision from his mind. Instead he fixed on some words he had read on a headstone that very day, and these he recited in his head:

> *Life is mostly froth and bubble,*
> *Two things stand like stone.*
> *Kindness in another's trouble,*
> *Courage in your own.*

He mulled over the words of the two women at the boarding house. There had been no compassion for the woman who had lost her daughter. Her secrets had been bandied about as though they had no mistakes of their own. Tobias was brought to mind of his own misdeeds, his own dark past. He would doubtless be condemned by many for the term of his natural life, without those people who stood in judgement ever knowing the facts.

His mind rested on Emma. He would be so proud when they

could spend time in each other's company in public without curious eyes and angry stares. It wouldn't be long until her mourning was over, and then they would get married. It warmed his heart.

Did Phoebe feel for their plight? Was that why she had invited him and Emma for morning tea, that they might share some small, cherished moments together away from sharp tongues? He was grateful, whatever the reason.

When he walked into the parlour, he was reminded of an angel. Emma was as close to any that he could imagine. It wasn't only her lovely face and gentle smile, but it was her head and her heart that made her like none other to him. She gave a smile that he knew she saved for him alone.

His heart picked up its rhythm and he had to remind himself that here was a house that was grieving. It wouldn't do to break out in a jig when someone dear to them had recently died. He was surprised the couple were "at home" for callers, since there had been a death in the family. Yet abiding by convention would never warm the heart like sharing company could.

'Good morning to you Tobias,' Rory greeted him at the door. They shook hands and Tobias scooted his chair so close to Emma's that the skirt of her gown grazed his hand. He intended to sit every bit as close to her as he could without actually sitting on the chair that she was on. He met her glance and didn't want to let it go. She smiled and looked down into her lap.

Phoebe giggled and began to pour the tea.

'You've baked my favourite, my dear,' Rory noted as he sat down to table.

Phoebe smiled as though it was the best compliment her husband could give.

'Would you expect anything less, Rory Ferguson?'

'I would not.'

The temptation was there. Emma's hand rested in her lap.

Tobias took the opportunity and covered her hand with one of his own. Now his heart was thumping like a bodhran.

'You know there is a rectory high tea in the church grounds?' Phoebe asked Emma.

'I did, but under the circumstances, I wasn't going to mention it to either you or Aunt Adelaide.'

Phoebe's smile was sad. 'In some ways we'll be grieving for the rest of our lives. What importance does wearing black for six months have?'

'Give me the sun on my face and the wind at my back, for life comes around only once that I can tell.'

Phoebe nodded. 'I agree with you, Tobias. And right now, keeping busy is what we must do,' even as her voice shook, she picked up the cake knife with determination. 'Let's hope the afternoon will be warm and sunny, so that we can sit on the lawn and look out at the harbour.'

Although Emma had told him very little about Euphemie, he had noticed her reticence to tell him what she had really been like. He gauged that Euphemie hadn't liked her lovely cousin, and had tried on more than one occasion to see her in hot water. Yet who would have motive for murder, and why?

After a second serving of cake, the two men went to stand by the fire. Rory began to pack his pipe. 'Leave the tea things be, Phoebe love. I'll clear the table later.'

'Do you think them too heavy for me?' Phoebe asked with a smile.

'In some months they might be,' he was grinning, blushing like a boy, 'so I'm getting into practice now.'

The young Irishman had made a friend of him, long before Tobias had ever earned his freedom. Whether it was because they were countrymen, Tobias didn't know, but he accepted it as genuine.

'Has the commandant learned anything noteworthy?' Tobias asked.

Rory shook his head and glanced at the women to see if they were engrossed in their own conversation before he spoke. The fire licked up towards the chimney. Embers crackled in the grate, hushing his words.

'Not that I've heard, but I can tell you that he has eyes and ears abroad for any information.' Tobias nodded. Rory went on, 'I didn't tell Phoebe how it happened. How could I be so unthinking? I said her sister had suffered a knock. Told the mother-in-law the same. It won't be me to tell them anything to the contrary either.' Rory shrugged. 'It was the best I could do.'

'It was the right thing to do,' Tobias gave him his assurance. 'Unfortunately even though I only told the surgeon the brief facts, it was more than enough. Maybe a lie would have been better than the barefaced truth.' Tobias put a distracted hand through his hair. Rory clapped Tobias soberly on the back.

'Someone had to do it. Nothing you could say would have sugar-coated it. It is what it is. There's nothing sweet in murder.'

The two men stood in silence for some moments. Tobias was glad when Rory changed the subject, putting a flame to his pipe and puffing a few times before he spoke.

'Seems a new officer has taken old Quinn's place.' Tobias waited and Rory went on, 'I heard you and he nearly had a run in the other day.'

'Aye,' Tobias conceded. 'You must be talking about Octavius Gray. He and I don't exactly get along.'

'He'd like to court your girl.'

'Would he now? I thought as much.' Anger flared inside him. He tamped it down.

'Easy on the eye, I think he said.'

'Well, you can tell him from me, she's already spoken for.'

'And her in mourning yet?'

Tobias felt his face flush. He would be damned if he let gossips rule his days. Then he spared a thought for Emma's reputation and conceded that it would take some time before he could court her openly.

Twelve

'When are we leaving?' Cecily wanted to know, and not for the first time that morning.

'We'll go presently.' Tobias fastened their few provisions at the front of the barge. The sun had only just begun to rise, and Tobias would be glad of the warmth. The day promised to be bright and clear, but right then the chill was sharp.

Cecily Quinn sat in the boat, impatient, watchful, hugging herself against the cutting breeze. A flock of seagulls bobbed like small buoys. She watched them dispassionately, pulling the black shawl tighter around the bones of her small frame.

'What are we waiting for?' Her voice was querulous over the sharp smack of the waves against the boat.

'We're waiting for Miss Colchester.'

'Why on earth are we waiting for Miss Colchester?' Cecily demanded, squinting up at him.

'She is coming to bid us a good journey,' Tobias answered cautiously. 'Perhaps because you're the mother-in-law she thought to have, she is extending you the courtesy of good manners,' he shrugged.

The planes of Cecily's face took on a placated look. 'Oh, how very kind it is of her,' Cecily smiled.

Tobias nodded and met her eye. 'She is the kindest young lady anyone could care to meet.'

'And she was going to marry my Gideon?' He heard her voice quaver.

He looked down and busied himself again. 'Aye, she was.'

'How did she come to meet Gideon?'

'I believe her aunt mentioned his name in a letter to Emma's mother as an …'

'Upstanding suitor?'

Tobias hesitated, finding words that were more appropriate than mere curses. There were none. 'I believe it was something like that.'

'A life cut short. I'll be eighty come the summer. My boy will never reach my age.'

Now, Quinn had been well over sixty, and considering the man had been a liar, thief and cold-blooded murderer, Tobias thought he had done well to live as long as he had, without some grudge bearer settling a score.

He looked at the sunrise over the water, and there coming down the road with the light at her back was Emma. She smiled when she greeted him.

'Good morning, Emma,' Tobias glanced at Cecily. He noticed her look of censure. That they called one another by their given names was a little untoward, but then this was not old England. This was a whole new world.

'Good morning Mistress Quinn,' Emma went to the barge and paid her respects.

'I only hope this young man will be careful,'

'You could be in no safer hands.'

'We'll break our journey at the Wheatsheaf Arms,' Tobias told Emma. 'And, if we don't waste any time we might be at The Folly before nightfall.' Tobias didn't want her concerned for his safety.

'The bed is made and the curtains are at the window,' Emma said quietly. 'They had been ready for a special night but I'm sure Mistress Quinn will be pleased for the comfort.'

He sighed, glancing at the small black clad figure sitting in the bobbing boat.

'There will be other cottages, Tobias. As long as we are together, nothing else matters. Quinn's Folly was never mine to have, just as I was never Gideon's. It's only right that it has come to pass this way.' The slow smile in her eyes begged him to understand. He nodded. She was right. He felt like a lad nursing disappointment.

'I will take Mistress Quinn to The Folly.'

'Do that, but please come home safely to me.'

'I'll be back before high tea in the parson's garden.' His gaze washed over her lovely features and settled on her clear grey eyes.

She waved them off moments too soon, and Tobias already missed her, even though she wasn't yet out of sight.

'I have decided to allow Miss Colchester to come and live with me at Wallis Plains.'

Tobias stilled the oars, his mouth falling slack. She went on, 'She was going to marry my son, after all. I'm sure there will be room for the both of us.'

Tobias's smile was tongue in cheek. Quinn's house was nothing like the modest cottage he thought the woman imagined.

'The girl doesn't need to live cheek by jowl with the surgeon and ... Adelaide, anymore.'

Tobias listened. But he had other ideas and they had nothing to do with Cecily Quinn. He settled on these as he drew the oars through the water. He smiled into the distance, aiming the boat towards the destination as he considered his future with Emma.

Water lapped the roots of the mangrove trees that lined the bank. A group of natives sat around a camp fire. The smell of wood smoke and coal-blackened meat—perhaps kangaroo—as the blacks watched the slow progress of the boat. A flash of red took his eye, and he started, dropping the oar. Cecily snorted and shifted in her sleep.

On the far bank, someone dressed as one of the soldiers of the crown moved on his haunches, hunkering a little closer to the warmth of the fire. Tobias couldn't help but stare at the group. He wondered why there was a redcoat amongst the natives. Socialising between soldiers and the blacks wasn't done.

Hairs on his arms rose like hackles but he couldn't for the life of him understand why. When the man turned to watch the passage of the barge through the water, Tobias failed to make out the face, and yet he seemed familiar. Tobias wondered at his unease. How easily the mind could play tricks. His memory had likely just been awoken by the sight of the red coat, because Gideon Quinn had been dead for months past.

Cecily slept sound, rocked by the rhythm of the boat against the lapping tide, oblivious to Tobias's momentary unease. He turned back to look for the man, but they had rounded a bend in the river, and the mangrove trees hid the camping natives from sight.

They stopped at the Wheatsheaf Arms. His shoulders needed a little time to recuperate after the repetition of rowing. Later he'd continue upriver plying the pole for a time instead. Right now he'd give his trembling muscles rest.

Cecily looked slightly miffed that they hadn't already arrived at their destination. She pursed her lips and remained silent, walking the distance from the shore to the public house, where she planted herself on the nearest upright chair, and proceeded to pack her pipe. She coughed and retched as the smoke hit her lungs. The hacking continued until she took a draught of ale, then settled to an occasional splutter as she sipped her tankard.

'Have you far to travel?' The publican wiped the counter with a dirty rag.

'We're headed to Wallis Plains. Thought we'd drop anchor and take a moment for refreshment before moving on.'

'You won't get there before dusk.'

'Sure, and don't I know it.' Tobias eased himself thankfully onto a stool.

'What takes you to Wallis Plains?' The curious pub owner wanted to know.

'I'm taking the lady over yonder to Quinn's Folly. A big sandstone house. Along the river it lies. Her son had it built on indentured labour. He was accidentally killed before he got to live there.'

'Oh, I know that place,' he whispered, his eyes growing large. He cast a glance in Cecily's direction. 'That's the haunted mansion you hear tell about.'

Tobias laughed.

The publican was adamant. 'I tell you, it's true. Jim drinks here regular like, and he's seen the apparition more than once.'

'Is he on his way home from the public house every time he sees this spectre?'

'No, not a bit of it,' the innkeeper reddened.

'Early one morning before cock's crow, the sun hadn't come up but he reckons it was nearly gone daybreak, and lo and behold there was this figure out in the mist, right in the middle of the field. Like a blooming scarecrow it was.'

Tobias quenched his thirst at a gulp and said nothing. He was brought to mind of young Allan Campbell, whose head Quinn had stoved in with a shovel not so many months before. And beyond the house, where Quinn had planned for crops, he had demanded that Tobias dig, and dig deep.

'Oh, there's been some funny goings on, I can tell you. Why the other night I was upstairs after closing time, when what do I hear but thumps thump thumps. It sounded like someone with a peg leg walking around down in the cellar. Well, I wasn't about to go and look. Scared out of my wits, I was. But next morning, sure enough, someone had climbed in through the cellar window, and had helped themselves to rum, bread and meat!' The publication shook his head, pushing the dirty dish rag away from himself. 'The sod had come and tapped the admiral beneath my very nose!'

'You never know who's around.'

'Well, if the blackguard comes a-calling again, I'll be sure to be on the ready. If the felon wants a measure, he can pay for it, along with everyone else.'

Tobias stretched and sighed. He didn't feel like going anywhere. They had only just arrived. But time was wasting.

'Better we don't tarry too long,' He nodded towards the river. 'There's danger enough in water, and that's with the light of day to go by.' He wasn't thinking of his own safety so much as the elderly lady sitting by the warmth of the fire.

'Well, if you change your mind, there are rooms upstairs with supper thrown in for nowt. Company sounds like a comfort. Might get myself a guard dog for peace of mind. The little woman is away at present, which is a shame because she's a fury with a rolling pin in her hand. Perhaps I'll put it beside the bed.' He laughed and his keg of a belly shook.

Tobias said farewell and he and Cecily walked out into the winter sunshine. Cecily had quaffed two tankards of ale, and seemed to drift from one side of the path to the other before they made it to the bank.

She lost a clog in the river and Tobias bent down to fish it out. She was a small woman, but to help the inebriated old soul into the barge was easier said than done and Tobias was only glad that they had left when they did otherwise he would have had to carry her to the boat.

The ale had made her drowsy. Without the prospect of more, she settled on the comfort of her pipe and puffed and coughed and hacked as they made their way downstream and away from the Wheatsheaf Arms.

Thirteen

The house was just as Tobias had last seen it. The convict labourers had all gone, and with them, the overseer. The garden, once started, was smothered by weeds. Thorny roses gave bare branches to the sky, and the master of the house was now master of none and lay resting in doubtful eternal peace beside the reeds that swayed along the river.

Cecily sat up to realise that they had reached their destination. As she looked up at the sandstone house, she let out a gasp of surprise. Her eyes widened at the house she intended to call home.

'This is it?' Cecily flapped, trying to stand up. The barge rocked. She put out a hand to steady herself. Tobias didn't blame her for her wonder at the place; he just wasn't about to share in her excitement. 'This is the place?' she demanded again.

Tobias nodded. He guessed she must have had to repeat it, just to make sure of the fact. When she knew it for a certainty, Cecily crowed at her good fortune. Tobias helped her from the boat and let her take his arm as they went to the front door. She was loud and enthusiastic at all she saw. She gave a curse in way of appreciation at the sconces fixed at either side of the archway, before she looked up at the heavy cedar-fronted entry. The door was all of seven foot high, and Cecily exclaimed at her son's genius, not realising that the skills of indentured men had created the marvel that was Quinn's Folly. Tobias had named it thus.

'Where does my son rest?' She stilled her hand upon the brass knocker.

He pointed to where the grass still struggled to grow. Tobias sat down on the porch step and waited for her to pay her respects.

When she returned, tears had run like scratches down her

white-powdered cheeks. She looked fatigued, older than when she had stepped from the boat.

'It has been a good many years since I saw him. We grew apart, but he was still my son. I never thought to see his end before my own. Now he will be close to me again until my end. Like he was as a tiny lad, always at my side.'

Tobias looked down at his feet. It was Cecily who deserved to have all this, and no one else. There were no words he could give her, so he merely nodded and opened the front door.

Upstairs, Tobias glanced over to the corner of the room, to the stolen rum taken from the government stores. He thought that if Cecily Quinn decided to indulge in a tipple, she'd be hard pressed to get out of bed the next morning. He was brought back to the present at the sound of her voice.

'You can stay here and work for me if you want to,' Cecily offered.

'You are going to need help, and I thank you for the offer, but I don't want the job.'

'Why not?' Cecily was crestfallen. The look on her face told him so.

'There are convicts aplenty who can work this place. There are free settlers who would be glad of the position for food and a place to lay their head, but it isn't for me. I've done as you wished, and have business to be about.'

This wasn't the plan Cecily had in mind, he knew. She wanted Emma to be her housemaid and sounding board and him to be her groundsman and jack-of-all-trades. Aye, he knew what the woman had in mind. Doubtless loneliness had a hand in it too.

'We can stay here the night, but then come morning I'm better off taking you back to the Wheatsheaf. You can board at the inn until there is suitable help found. I'll ask the publican if he knows of a likely worker.'

'I'm not going back there.' Cecily was petulant. 'We brought flour, tea, salt mutton and sugar. There's wood on the pile and water in the creek. This was to be Gideon's home,' she began to sniffle. 'Now he has left it to me.'

Tobias didn't think that Quinn would willingly have given anything to anyone, but wasn't about to tell her so. The woman's safety was pressing.

'What if some calamity befalls you? It's a hard man that leaves an elderly lady to her fate.'

'Then stay here and work for me,' she pleaded. 'I'll let you make a room above the stables.'

His smile was dry. *You're all kindness ...*

Tobias stopped her offer with a gesture of his hand. 'I'll slave for no man except the family I hope I'm eventually blessed with. I'm sorry Mistress Quinn, but that's my decision and I won't be changing it.'

He saw her take some coin from her purse, which she held out to him as payment. He shook his head and she dropped the money back and drew it shut. 'I'll bid you good night now Mistress Quinn. I trust you have everything you need?'

'I do.'

'I was going to leave first thing, but tomorrow I'll make sure of your comfort and see what I can do about the place in the way of odd jobs. But it's an early start I'll be getting the morning after. I'll be gone by cock's crow.'

'Thank you for everything you've done.' Her tone was grudging, but her thanks was not.

He needed no more payment than that.

Tobias lit a fire in the grate and collected two pails of water from the creek to sit them in the house. Quinn's mother took a chair from the kitchen and sat before the blaze he made for her, puffing like a bellows on the tiny clay pipe in her wizened mouth. Once white, the pipe was stained brown with tobacco, dark as the few stumps that bit down upon it. She looked truculent, thrusting out her lower lip. She glowered in his direction more than once, but said nothing. She swung the kettle of water over the fire and waited for it to boil.

It was a simple meal of salt mutton and river water that Tobias ate alone in the stable. The bed was no more than he had expected. Still, he had slept on worse than mouldy straw before this. There were no shackles now that tied him to the next miserable soul beside him. He piled the dry fodder into the corner, and thought of Emma. Yet he was so tired that he knew that not even thoughts of his darling would keep him awake.

Before he prepared to sleep, he decided to go to the house. He wanted to make sure one last time that the woman was settled for the night. She wasn't his ma, but someone had to look out for her.

Tobias walked up the steps and onto the porch. He saw her through the window and stopped suddenly, his hands at his side. She had dressed up in some kind of cheap finery, all satin, lace and frills. The low bodice showed more tired flesh than Tobias wanted to see. Her cheeks were stained bright with rouge. She was smiling as though she spoke to some imaginary visitor, preening as she gestured about her like some grand hostess.

He was embarrassed by the charade. Saddened to witness the lonely sight. It came to Tobias keenly that he had a lot to be thankful for. Let Cecily keep her castle and gain some small happiness from it while she might. Tobias headed for the stable.

Fourteen

Emma closed the cottage gate. The late winter afternoon was just as Phoebe had hoped for the parson's lawn party. Yet it hardly mattered what the weather was like because Tobias would soon be home.

Phoebe waved to her from the parsonage gate. Tables and chairs dotted the lawn.

'Mama and Papa? They aren't coming?' Phoebe's face fell a little. 'Perhaps I shouldn't be here either?'

'Phoebe, you honour Euphemie with every thought you spare. Your parents are together beside the fire, keeping one another company. I say we take tea.'

'Has Mr. Freeman arrived back?'

'I don't know,' Emma found that she was blushing.

'But you wait with anticipation?' Phoebe asked the question, yet smiled knowingly. Emma dipped her head to hide the heat of her cheeks.

'Someone else has been waiting for you. You have more than one admirer, Emma. Can you guess who? I don't mean Commandant Morisset, either,' Phoebe teased. 'That poor man knows he doesn't stand a chance with you.'

'Perhaps you might focus on knitting bootees, Phoebe, instead of ... ' Emma searched for the words.

'Keeping score of my cousin's string of suitors?' Phoebe asked archly.

'Exactly so, Phoebe,' Emma laughed.

The two joined arms and Phoebe whispered, 'Why, speak of the Devil himself, here he is now, and a handsome one at that.'

'Phoebe, please desist teasing me,' Emma hissed, mock severity on her features.

It didn't wipe the smile off Phoebe's face.

'Miss Colchester.' The officer bowed deeply.

'Officer Gray.' Emma saw a gleam in the man's eye. There was more than polite interest in the look he gave her. She saw the invitation before she glanced away. Let that dissuade him.

'Allow me to extend a good afternoon to you, Mrs. Ferguson.'

'Officer Gray.' Phoebe inclined her head. 'We have a lovely afternoon to share high tea on the lawn. I hope you will sample the cake I made?'

'I certainly shall. And you, Miss Colchester, did you bake?'

'I'm afraid not.'

'Pity, I should enjoy sampling some of your delights.'

Emma glanced at Phoebe. Her cousin choked back laughter.

Emma noted that the three of them didn't go unnoticed by landlady of the guest house. Mistress McGuiness's eyes followed them with more interest than she did the spread.

'I must admit that I prefer to roll bandages and bathe wounds at the hospital. I think my uncle enjoys our walks to and from the hospital as much as I do.'

'I'm sure my father thinks Emma could well have been a doctor herself,' Phoebe praised her. 'Mama and I prefer to sew and bake.'

'I must give you my condolences on your loss, Mrs. Ferguson.'

'Thank you, Officer Gray. It has been a terrible shock for us all.'

'The law is on our side. Never fear, but there will be a reckoning. Nothing will bring your beloved sister back, but justice will be served. I give you my word on that.'

'I trust you are correct, Officer Gray,' Emma said.

'I'll be at the forefront of the investigation in finding the culprit.'

They walked to a group of chairs beneath the dappled sun of a shading tree. 'Ladies, please allow me to get you some refreshments,' Octavius Gray gave a slight bow before he walked away.

'It is a pity that there are three eligible bachelors, and yet only one of you. Tobias Freeman, Officer Gray, and Commandant Morisset,' Phoebe sighed, counting the gentlemen off on one hand.

'There is only one man I love,' Emma reminded her cousin.

'Well, Miss Colchester, you'd better be about telling me who he is,' Tobias startled both girls. Emma laughed up at him.

'I'm going to have a few words in the ear of this suitor,' he smiled.

Emma wanted to stand close enough to feel his warmth. Instead she let him have her smile.

Octavius Gray returned with two tea cups filled nearly to the brim with scalding tea. He threw a hot look in Tobias's direction before he set them down.

Phoebe glanced at both the men, sizing up the situation. She began, 'Officer Gray, have you gentlemen been given an introduction?'

'We have had an introduction of sorts,' the officer admitted, giving Tobias a curt nod. Tobias said not a word. Emma and Phoebe exchanged worried looks in each other's direction.

'Officer Gray, come and let me point out the baking I hope to tempt you with. My dear husband Rory is on duty and I cannot take him a morsel, so perhaps you will allow me to spoil you?'

Sweet Phoebe diplomatically steered Octavius Gray away from trouble. The irritation she had seen flash over Tobias's face mirrored the steel in the officer's own. It seemed that Octavius Gray thought no more of Mr. Freeman than Tobias did of him.

Tobias folded his arms and planted his feet. He cast a dark look in the direction of Octavius Gray before he looked back to Emma.

She wanted to tell him that there was no competition, that he had no reason to fear that she would look at the officer above him. Instead she asked, 'How did you fare with Cecily Quinn?'

'She wanted me to stay and work for her. Not just myself but you, and she says you have a home there with her, if you like.'

'Would you consider it?'

Tobias shook his head. 'Not unless you were lady of the house. While ever there's breath in my body, Emma, you're the only one I want to serve.'

Emma reached out to touch his hand just as Octavius Gray returned. He made a point to look askance at her mourning clothes as she unclasped Tobias's hand.

'I will bid you good afternoon, Miss Colchester,' Officer Gray's voice was cool. He cut a sharp nod in Tobias's direction, 'Good day to you, sir.'

Tobias didn't bother with cordiality at all. He said not a word.

Phoebe stopped short at the table.

'Officer Gray didn't stay very long.'

Tobias told her honestly, 'Aye, well maybe he knew I would have liked to pan him out.'

Fifteen

The owner of the boarding house was a dab hand with the rolling pin, and the steak and oyster pie had been no exception. Sure, and as if he needed a second helping. But the woman had told him that since he was the only one boarding at present, the pudding would certainly go to waste if he didn't tackle *'another wee mouthful.'*

He hadn't needed to be encouraged twice.

When he had returned from Wallis Plains he was beat, glad to sit under the trees with Emma, even if it meant he had to put up with Octavius Gray. Yet at least he had been able to forget all about Cecily Quinn.

Now he imagined she was calling out to him from the other side of the door. He forgot he was in the boarding house on clean linen. He drifted off again, not wanting to be bothered by the woman yet a while. Since she had stepped off the brig she hadn't given him a moment's peace, and here she was banging on the door of his room, telling him she needed to speak to him. That he had to get up.

It was no use. The woman wouldn't go away. Tobias sighed and sat up, rising from the edge of the bed to pull up his breeches. He rolled his knuckles over his eyes and blinked at the day. Looking out of the window he saw that it must have been near noon. Then the banging started again. Tobias pulled open the door.

He was confronted with three redcoats, one of whom was Octavius Gray. 'Top of the morning to you,' Gray quipped, the Irish brogue he aped at odds with his demeanour. There was a smile of triumph, and Tobias knew that something was very wrong. His stomach clenched into a fist of unease.

'What's the problem?' Tobias ignored the slur. The smile that stretched across Gray's face broadened. Unease tripped up Tobias's spine.

'Why, sir that's what we've come here for, in the hope that you can help us. You see, an elderly lady by the name of Cecily Quinn was found dead in her deceased son's house. To our knowledge sir, you were the last person who saw her alive.'

Tobias stared. He searched the faces of each of the three men. He saw the truth of the statement in their eyes. For long moments Tobias said nothing. He held out empty hands, looking from one to another. 'I've done nothing.'

His sincerity won a chuckle from Octavius Gray. 'I thought you'd say that. Still, that's what we're going to find out; whether you killed a woman in cold blood or not.'

Tobias felt the life drain from his body. His new identity fell away like a shadow, and he became a convict again, a felon with neither name nor dignity. He was a man without power against the crown.

'You can come with us, Mr. Freeman. But how much longer you have your freedom, is anyone's guess.'

There was nothing that could be said in his defence. If Tobias had no witness, no one to lend credibility to his words, then his innocence was meaningless. No magistrate would accept the words of a man without a defence, especially when the man was a recently convicted felon, albeit a freed one.

Hope drained away just like water through oatmeal, and with it the strength in his frame. Tobias stumbled over his feet going down the stairs of the boarding house, but a soldier on either side stopped his fall.

Yet although his world was falling from beneath his feet, when he walked out into the winter sun, it still continued to be a beautiful day. He wondered how many more such as this he would be granted.

Townspeople lined the road. On either side they stood and gaped, open mouthed at the spectacle, convicts and free settlers alike. No bell chimed. No birds broke the sound of his boots trudging the path. And the only movement he noticed was the shadow of himself in the dirt as it walked at his side.

On their cottage stoop stood Kevin and Mary. He read the fear and sadness in their faces. As they approached, Kevin waited, reaching out with pity in his eyes. There was no jest or quip from the Cockney this day, no laugh in the sunburned face.

Kevin stepped before the soldiers to clap him upon the back. 'Bless you, Toby.'

He would have heard, just as all the townsfolk had, the gossip of the old woman's death. Yet Kevin would not believe a word of the loud whispers that he had listened to, Tobias knew, because the man knew him for who he was.

'Tobias!' It was the only voice he longed for, and all that he held dear. He pulled away from the soldiers. They stopped beside him and he waited for her; for Emma, running down the road.

Her eyes were wide. Tears ran down her face, and for the first time, for the very first time since he had known her, Emma forgot that she was a lady. She appeared to care nothing for any opinion around her. She looked neither left nor right, only at him, and it almost broke him to see her this way. His breath hitched in his throat.

'Emma,' his voice was raw.

Even the soldiers stepped aside in deference and looked away, before she flung herself into his arms. He heard her sob, and he told himself that was why his own eyes filled with unshed tears.

He was worried for her reputation. 'Emma, you were engaged to Quinn and you're in mourning, still. Leave go of me, or everyone will know.'

She looked up at him with so much love and sadness. 'It matters not to me.' With that, he kissed her full on her mouth, for the whole of the colony to bear witness to.

'Come on, mate,' one of the soldiers said, taking him by the arm again. 'Time to go.'

Tobias let them lead him into the gaol with the little dignity as he could muster.

'Aye,' he said aloud, though he spoke only to himself. 'The whole world may know I love her now. I care naught.'

✠

Katy stood beside the commandant as the soldiers took Tobias away. She looked up at him, with his black curls and handsome face. He smelled sweet like Parson's flower garden. She thought she might marry him one day. He would look at her just like Tobias looked at Miss Colchester, and there would be a fairy-tale in it.

But this was sad, and the commandant was sad, she could tell. He stood there in his coat with the buttons all shined up, but there was no smile on his face. Nearly every time he saw Katy, he smiled, but when she stared up at him and he looked down at her, she was miserable too.

The commandant always told everyone what to do, so why did he let Miss Colchester cry like that? Why did he let Tobias get taken away by the soldiers to the gaol? She remembered the humbug he had whipped from somewhere inside his coat like a conjurer. That had made her smile, so why did he stand there without a word to those redcoats grabbing hold of Tobias?

Then she remembered something, and like a flash of warmth that came from right down inside her, Katy knew what to do. She wriggled through the crowd to get to the front door of their cottage, pushing open the door.

Buried down where she had left it, between mattress and wattle and daub wall, was the scarlet ribbon. She grabbed for it. She barely even glanced at her treasure, because now it wasn't of any use to her at all.

She ran up to the commandant as he made to walk away. She pulled at his hand and he looked down at her as though he didn't see her. Katy reached up to push the scrap of satin inside his hand. He opened his palm and touched it and at first she thought he was angry, and then, that he might well cry too.

Katy bit her lip. The commandant looked so deeply into her eyes, then, and Katy read what they said: *Thank you, Katy, for giving me my ribbon back.* Then, he did just what she had hoped for.

He smiled.

Sixteen

Commandant Morisset looked at the scrap of ribbon on his desk. It drew his eyes like a cut drew blood. Little Katy had thought he wanted it, but in fact he almost loathed it. Every time he looked at it he imagined he saw the decaying corpse of the surgeon's daughter. Not as she had been in life, but as she had stared up sightlessly in death.

The young woman who had tried to pay him court, and whom he had wanted nothing to do with. The scarlet satin was just a slip of a thing, but it was a reminder of a life lived in vain and lost. It was a reminder of his guilt.

Why hadn't he escorted her to her parent's door on the night she had accosted him? Why hadn't he cared enough to show her that respect, at least? She had hidden in the darkness like some strumpet waiting for business. She had even tried to drape herself over him as he made to bid her good evening and walk away. The display had embarrassed him, angered him even. He frowned as he tried to remember her name. He couldn't even recall it. He hadn't owed her his affection, but he would have liked to give her a name.

Sighing, he left the barracks. It was one of those days that wearied the soul. Not even the sun could be bothered to shine. But the waves were constant, and rolled to the shore to lap the sands at his restless feet.

'Commandant Morisset?' He swung around.

Perhaps Miss Colchester was restive too. 'Miss Colchester, you startled me. I was far away, I must admit.'

'I have been sitting with Mr. Freeman. You appear homesick.'

He smiled and shrugged, looking towards the harbour, towards further shores. 'Sometimes, I am indeed. Perhaps one day I will travel home. Who knows. I shan't stay here in Newcastle forever, I don't think.' Emma nodded.

'Your heart is here,' he commented. Emma smiled sadly. It was true.

'First cell on the right,' he tried to make a joke of it, and failed. 'I'm sorry, Miss Colchester. It's no laughing matter.'

'No, it isn't, but it you're correct regarding where my heart resides. I'm not offended. I know you mean no disrespect.'

He shook his head at the futility of the situation. 'I only hope that Tobias Freeman's innocence is brought to light.' He turned to her in earnest. 'I don't for one moment think that he murdered Cecily Quinn in cold blood.' He held out his hands, as empty and clueless as he was. 'All I do know is that he was the last person known to have seen her alive. Yet every deed I have seen or heard of in that man tells me that he's a man with integrity. He no more throttled Cecily Quinn than he did your departed cousin.'

She shot him a look. 'Wasn't she hit upon the head? Rory Ferguson said she had been struck down.'

The commandant hesitated. He had put his foot in it again, and he wondered what Tobias Freeman had told the family. Ferguson had omitted the truth. Did being done in with a dustpan sound better than throttled by a braid?

'No, I'm afraid that's not correct.' He cleared his throat. 'It was strangulation on both counts.'

She put a hand over her mouth.

'I'm sorry.' It was a lame apology for thoughtless speaking.

'Such a horrible deed,' she whispered.

'May justice be served.'

They looked out at the harbour for long moments. The afternoon had grown sleepy, preparing for dusk. The commandant walked Emma in the direction of her uncle's house, as he should have done on the night not so long ago for Miss Colchester's cousin.

If there was a God in heaven He might forgive him for caring so little for one of His creatures on that fateful night. He knew he couldn't have saved Cecily Quinn from death, but he might have saved the surgeon's daughter.

Surely there had to be a correlation in the demise of the women who had been killed? Whoever had done it had gone far afield. Surely it had been someone with transport, since Wallis Plains was a good day's journey. Obviously it was no indentured man, because the convicts had to account for their whereabouts too many times in one day, with five roll calls in all. Who else but a free man would have mode of conveyance and time on his hands? A free man, but not Freeman, surely?

Both women had met the same end. A labourer looking for work had found Cecily Quinn on the bedroom floor. She had dropped where she stood. The commandant might have thought she had been entertaining a gentleman but for the fact that she would have been eighty if she was a day. Could one and the same murderer have killed both women? He couldn't think where to begin his search for answers.

When the commandant arrived back at the barracks he said as much to Octavius Gray; the officer shook his head.

'I believe the murderer is behind bars as we speak,' Gray attested. 'I don't believe it.'

'Why not? He was with the old woman on the evening that she died. He had taken her down the Hunter River just days before and drank a draught with the innkeeper before they traveled on.'

'And the surgeon's daughter? What of her? It could have been an unrelated crime.' Octavius Gray smirked. 'Do you try to hand me a red herring, sir?'

'Not at all, why?'

'The mode of death was so startlingly alike. Braids wrapped around the neck and pulled tight the way a woman closes her purse. Now, Freeman was here when the girl went missing, and he was with the old woman in Wallis Plains when she was done to death. Tobias Freeman is the target, and we, sir are the arrow.'

Commandant Morisset saw the officer with new understanding.

'Regarding the death of those women, I believe you are wrong. Way off the mark, for all that it looks like the only convincing story. But I'll tell you something else for nothing: if you think that hanging Tobias Freeman by the neck will get you any closer to courting Emma Colchester, you are wrong again.'

Octavius Gray said nothing and now the commandant offered a humourless smile as he made to walk away.

'And now, I know I have hit the target, on one score at least.'

Octavius Gray bridled. 'What if he is the cold-blooded scoundrel that I think he is? Those two murders are not his first. I have found that he was only recently pardoned for his crimes, but everyone knows that old habits are hard to silence. The man is a murderer, sir.'

'As far as I am concerned, Tobias Freeman is innocent until we find evidence to the contrary. Show me the proof, Gray and I will tie the noose for him myself. But until I have evidence, until he is given a fair trial, I know no more than you do.'

The commandant strode away without a backward glance. Octavius Gray was getting under his skin. The man was like sand upon the bed linen.

But the officer knew, just as well as he did, that unless someone came forward with the truth to the contrary Tobias Freeman would be hanged by the neck until he was dead.

Seventeen

'Emma! Emma, where are you?'

Emma emerged from the outhouse. Aunt Adelaide stood by the garden gate, looking up and down the street. Taking in the woman's angry expression, Emma prepared to listen to the querulous complaints of the overwrought woman.

'I wondered where you could have gone.'

Emma exercised patience. 'No reason to worry Aunt Adelaide, as you see, I'm still here. I'll walk up to the hospital later, and come home with Uncle George, but you'll be all right, because Matilda will be here with you.'

Matilda was the servant in every sense of the word a convict to the crown as well as to her aunt and uncle. Her aunt wasn't content with the consolation. She made a scornful noise.

'They're all the same.'

Emma prepared for the onslaught. Her aunt looked at her pointedly. 'You know who I'm talking about of course.' She scowled, and flung her hand towards the colony. 'Convicts. Thieves, murderers the lot.'

Emma sighed and looked away. The path was barred by her aunt, standing firmly between her and the cottage. She had heard this before, this rant, and wanted only to rid herself of the never-ending finger of shame pointed at her by Aunt Adelaide.

'Now don't look at me like that, my girl. I'm speaking of Tobias Freeman, and well you know it.'

'I do, and I don't care to hear of your opinion any more.'

Aunt Adelaide gulped on Emma's words. They caught in her aunt's throat like a fish bone. Words momentarily failed her.

'I have lost my daughter to a heartless devil, and you tell me you don't want to hear it? I live and breathe the horror of what that girl suffered in her last moments, and you dare to say that you don't care to know?' The stabbing finger came so close to Emma's face that she had to turn her head for fear of being struck.

'I didn't mean that I have no care for your loss, Aunt Adelaide.' The last days had been a nightmare for Emma too. 'The man I love has been convicted of ... '

Her aunt's laugh was a horrible thing. It was goading and it was cruel. 'Oh, I know,' she nodded with ferocious glee.

Emma took a step back. Aunt Adelaide took another closer.

'I know what he was convicted of. And if he killed Cecily, how do you know he didn't kill my darling Euphemie as well? And you tell me that he is the man you love? How can you love someone like that?' She looked at Emma as though unable to comprehend how stupid her niece was. 'Do you forget that the man was a felon?'

Emma had nothing to say. Warm tears pooled in her eyes to spill from her lashes and down her cheeks.

'Tobias is not a murderer.' It was a weak argument.

'Everyone in the colony is convinced that he did it,' her aunt spoke to her as if she was a simpleton. 'The commandant gave him a ticket of leave, but by the same token, who do you think saw to his arrest? Yes, that's right; it was Commandant Morisset. Yet you will walk to the gaol like the naive girl you are, to visit him like some hospital invalid, as though he is a man convicted of a crime he didn't commit. Well, I tell you that he did.'

'How do you know?' Emma demanded. 'How *can* you know?'

Her aunt hit her breast with assurance. As though it was the Bible she gave her oath upon. 'I feel it in my heart.' Her aunt began to cry.

Emma reached out to comfort her aunt but was struck away.

'Don't think that you can just make a fool of us, gallivanting after him like you have been.' The finger was drawn out again. 'I tell you now that if you continue to visit him in the constabulary gaol, then you leave this house.'

Emma stared, dumbstruck.

'That's right, you heard me. You can pick up your bags and get out. I don't care where you go.'

Aunt Adelaide turned and strode away, her skirt dragging at the lavender hedge. It smelled bitter. Emma wondered where on earth she could go. Where could she call home? She would not give Tobias up. She stared around her at the houses on the street.

Perhaps Mrs. Brown, the rector's wife would give her refuge, or yet, her cousin Phoebe. But even dear Phoebe might yet abandon her, if not for her own beliefs, then perhaps for her mother's.

In some ways Emma prayed that Tobias's trial would be soon, in the hope that he would be freed. Yet at the same time, she had sense enough to realise that the longer he waited for his time in court, the more chance there was of learning the truth, of finding the person responsible for the acts.

She recalled the night before Phoebe was married.

There had been a full moon and a clear sky. Voices just along the road further up the hill. Emma had listened. A familiar voice. It was Euphemie. Emma had stayed her hand giving scraps to the dog, thinking that her cousin had called to her from across the street. Emma made to walk towards her, then stopped.

It wasn't Emma that Euphemie was entreating, but Tobias. Her tone was cajoling, petulant. Emma couldn't hear the words, but she made out Euphemie put a waylaying hand on Tobias. Emma stood stock-still. Then came the sound of other voices spilling out of the public house. Emma went back inside the cottage, wondering what on earth Euphemie had been doing, and what part in it Tobias played, however seemingly unwillingly.

'*Tobias is not a murderer.*'

That was what she had said to her aunt. But as definite as

she was in her belief of Tobias, there was the fact that Tobias was one of the last people to have seen Euphemie alive. And then there was Cecily Quinn. What significance had Euphemie's interlude had in it all?

That he had killed the farmer had been an accident, he had told her himself, and yet what if the story he had told her had only been the tale he had wanted her to hear? What if the man had not struck his head on the hearth as he fell, but had in fact died in a far more violent struggle?

'Can you not see the blood on my hands?'

This had been his own admission. Was his past only what he chose to tell her? Emma put her head in her hands. She was ashamed of herself for having so little faith in the man she loved. Disgraced that as he sat in a gaol cell believing in her and their love, she doubted him even still.

Emma didn't go back inside the cottage. Instead she went in the direction of the parsonage. Mrs. Brown was always ready to boil the kettle, and if it wasn't refreshment Emma needed, it was friendship.

Eighteen

Jim groomed the mare. He mulled over what had been going on in Wallis Plains of late, and shivered. What he had seen weighed heavily on his shoulders. It was too hard a yoke for him to bear. As he considered what to do, he knew that what the publican urged him to do was right.

Although he worked as a timber cutter, Jim liked to think he was a top-notch handyman. He could turn his hand to most tasks with a certain degree of success, so that when he was paid for a job well done, he reckoned he deserved a pint or two at the inn. A pint or two was usually half a dozen more than what he told himself his quota was.

And on an aside, as far as he was concerned, if the innkeeper wasn't so steep with the price of his liquor, then the thief wouldn't have felt the need to help himself to a tipple of rum from the barrels in the tavern cellar in the first place. He couldn't really blame the robber wanting a cheap night out.

'I've barred the cellar window,' the publican had told him and Tam.

Jim had heard tell that ghosts could materialise through bricks and mortar. Still, Jim had a chuckle to himself as the publican told him the story of the ghost in the cellar.

'Since when do ghosts drink spirits?' Tam wanted to know. He had a good point, there. 'You say the spirit used the cup sitting on top of the barrel. But if it was a ghost,' he reasoned, 'why would he need to use a cup? A ghost is dead and has no body. The rum would have poured in one end and ran out the other.' Tam laughed along with Jim. The innkeeper didn't.

'It put my hackles up, that's certain. You've seen the ghost yourself, haven't you Jim?'

'True as I'm sitting on this stool,' Jim nodded, setting down his tankard with conviction. 'A faceless apparition, it was. Blood from the neck of his shirt to the string of his breeches.'

'Och, aye, and soon you'll be saying he climbed upon a headless horse in dead of night.'

A little the worse for wear, Jim grew cantankerous at the guffaws of laughter when they were turned upon him.

'If you come across it you won't be laughing, I'll give you that for nothing. I never want to see the thing again. It was pure evil that I saw, and there's nothing before or since that I've encountered that has been so close to the Devil.'

Scottish Tam had stopped laughing. Jim saw him shiver. Like unease just put a hand on his back. But Jim was sullen now, and brooded over his ale.

'Never sulk now Jim,' the innkeeper coaxed. 'I happen to have some good news for you.' Jim's ears pricked. The publican went on, 'Yesterday a gentleman and an old woman were making their way down river to that big house. Today he stopped in again and asked if I knew of anyone looking for work. I told him I knew just the one. Seems the woman needs a Jack-of-all-trades to look after the place. She hoped he'd work for her, but he didn't want to do it. She's there on her own. Said I'd let you know the moment I spoke to you.'

'I'll take it' Tam volunteered.

'You'll do nothing of the sort, Tam McNab.'

'Aye, well maybe she'll need the two of us,' Tam reasoned. 'I could serve as her butler.' He assumed a pompous air. Tam and the publican chuckled, but not Jim.

'If she does, Tam, I'll be sure to let you know. I'm going to head there directly.'

'You'll scare the bloomers off the old duck,' Tam laughed. 'It'll be close to dark by the time you get there.'

Jim could tell that Tam hankered for the easy-sounding work, but Jim was greedy for the opportunity of employment like this. He'd need the money if he was going to marry Polly. Who knew, perhaps the old girl would need a housemaid. He reckoned she'd be sure to need a female's hand about the place, so after he went to see the woman, he'd go and tell Polly.

Jim got down from the stool and headed for the door. 'I'll let you know how I get on,' he had told Tam, thanking the innkeeper on the way out.

He supposed he felt a bit bad that the innkeeper had put in a good word for him, mentioning his name to the traveler, especially since Tam was every bit as keen. Tam would be glad of any work that was easier than felling timber, fearful of blacks with spears as they were. The wiry Scotsman wasn't getting any younger, either. Jim would mention his name to the old girl. Who knew, with a house like that, she was bound to have plenty of money.

As he began to walk, the rain started. First intermittent drops, they grew closer together, heavier and faster, so that by the time he reached the front door of the big house he was soaked by the downpour. He called out through the already open door.

There weren't any tea things set out on the big cedar table. Jim eyed the piece of furniture as he would a beautiful woman. Wanted to stroke the gleaming timber. He liked making knick-knacks from wood, but had never seen anything so grand as this.

Jim put his head around the door to peer in. No pot hung over the fireplace in the kitchen; odd, for the time of day. He called out again but couldn't make himself heard over the din of the rain hammering down. He ventured inside, to stand hesitantly by the open door.

The blokes had been right; he should have waited until daylight, but he was here now, and he hadn't trusted Tam not to worm his way into the job before he could make himself known.

It was growing darker, and as he twisted his hat in his hands, he wondered what to do. He scratched his head and thought of his future with Polly. He pulled his hat back down upon his head and made to turn away into the dusk, only to pull it off again and turn back. He headed up the stairs, craning his neck to see if the old girl was there. There was no time like the present.

He noticed that the staircase was also cedar, and was well made at that. Not a sag or squeak to be heard from the boards as he mounted them tentatively. It was dim when he looked down the long hallway, even though the doors on the landing were opened and the windows were pretty big.

He was glad that the rain was making such an unholy racket. If he found the old lady asleep on her bed, he would creep away until morning and save himself the scolding he might get. But he was unnerved, walking through the quiet house, an unwelcome stranger that he was. He found that he was creeping up the hallway on his tiptoes.

When he first heard the noise, he was relieved. He made ready to call out. But when the gasping continued, Jim found himself rigid with fear. His feet were like lead. He could barely move. He was being ridiculous, but still he was afraid. Instinctively he made for safety. Even as he did, he asked himself what he thought he was about. The woman might need help. She might have swallowed a pearl from her choker.

Jim's instincts weren't so sure.

To his left there was an open door. He turned for it. A voice momentarily stopped him in his tracks.

'Strumpet! Strumpet no more!'

Jim's heart banged like a mallet. He could barely hear for the blood rushing in his ears. His mouth was hanging open. His chest heaved with the locomotion of his fear. Afraid of the smallest sound escaping his lips, he pulled up short at the room on his right. Because the rain had eased, and because he was a coward and didn't think he'd make it downstairs, he dragged himself to the open door and hid behind it. It was then that he realised that the gurgling in the next room had ceased.

If he died, Polly would never know he had intended to ask for her hand. If he was a man of learning he could pencil his love a note and put it in his waistcoat should he perish. As it was, he could neither read nor write!

There came the sound of a gentleman's boots on the hardwood floor. They approached, and the sweat fell off Jim like runnels down a gutter. Perspiration dripped into his eyes to sting. He dared not even blink it away, but stood rooted to the floor, sure the smell of his fear would betray him.

The footsteps were upon him. His legs began to buckle and shake. The flash of a red coat came into his vision for just an instant, and as the man looked beyond Jim and glanced into the room on his way past, he saw a face like none he had encountered before.

A glimpse was enough for him to see that the redcoat was maimed beyond all decency. Jim knew then, without a moment's doubt, that this was the apparition he had seen out in the open field. Only this was no spectre.

The footfalls receded. He heard the door close, and the rain fell down again in torrents.

Sweat ran down the length of his spine. It made it to the cinch of his breeches and down the crack of his backside. It was some time before he moved from behind the door, wanting only to escape. But then he glanced toward the next room and saw the vague glow of a candle.

Temptation got the better of him. He craned his neck around the doorway. There on the floor was an elderly woman. Dressed like a harpy, a look of horror still painted her face. A livid tongue pointed accusation. Grey stringy plaits were wrapped tight around her neck.

Jim spun away. He was going to be sick. He heaved and felt his innards quake as he left the innkeeper's ale on the floor. It left a sour taste in his mouth.

He stood upright and wiped his streaming mouth and eyes. A taper burned on the dresser. A lifetime of care with candles told him to snuff it out, but he left the candle burning and made his way down the stairs on stumbling legs. If the house burned to the ground it would be no bad thing.

He listened for the monster that had done the grisly deed, hesitating at every turn. It wasn't until he was well away of the place that Jim began to run.

He ran as if the Devil was on his heels.

He stopped behind the cover of a gum to wait and to listen. He peered all around into the darkness and saw nothing. The murderer could be anywhere, behind or ahead of him. Jim lurched pell-mell in the direction of the Wheatsheaf Arms.

It took ages to get there. His lungs felt fit to bursting, and his throat burned like bushfire, even though the night was cool. He had never run so far or so fast in the whole of his life. The innkeeper was about to shut up shop. Jim struggled to call out. His chest heaved painfully as he cried out.

'Don't close the door!'

The man peered around in the darkness, candle in hand. The lantern was swung in one direction, and then the other. The man took a step backwards. Jim pushed past the publican. The man was more than a little spooked.

'Jim?' The owner of the tavern squinted into the darkness.

'Aye.'

'I've seen you desperate for a pint many a time, but never so sorely as now,' the innkeeper chuckled, perplexed. 'It's closing time, man. You'll have to wait to slake your thirst until the morrow.'

But Jim barged past, dragging the chill night with him. 'Steady on now Jim!' The innkeeper was almost knocked off balance.

Jim grabbed the innkeeper. Pulled him inside.

'What are you up to?' The man shook off Jim's hands. He was beginning to get his hackles up.

'Murder. There's been murder. The old woman's dead and I was there.'

'I think you'd better repeat yourself. You're not making an ounce of sense.'

Jim collapsed onto a stool, fighting to quiet his breathing.

'Here, have this,' the innkeeper urged. He pushed a measure of rum towards Jim.

'Lock the door,' Jim told him. He thought for a moment he heard something outside. A rustle or footfall perhaps? He went to the door and barred it himself.

'Are you going to hurry up and tell me what all this ruckus is? I'd like to be about my bed.'

'I'm staying with you.' Jim was adamant.

The innkeeper raised his brows, bemused. 'I beg to differ.'

'I'll not step foot from this hearth until the sun's in the sky, and even then, I'm doubtful.'

'Have you the means for lodging?'

'Aye, I do, but I don't need a bed. It's beside the fire I'll lay where I can hear any noises.'

The innkeeper chuckled. 'I might as well pour myself a measure as well. I fear it'll be a long story in the telling.'

Jim shook his head, pointing at the tavern keeper. 'There's a monster outside the door, and I've seen it with my own eyes. Aye, you may smile, but I tell you, I saw evil this night and I'm lucky to have escaped with my life.'

'Did this monster look anything like the ghost out in the field?' The publican tried not to smile, but failed.

'The very same,' he breathed, 'and I tell you, it's no spirit.'

The publican tried to calm him, as though Jim was some poor mad beggar who'd lost his wits.

'I was in that house tonight when murder was done. I saw the murderer who did it and the woman he claimed, and I'm telling you now, bolt your doors and windows, for I'll not leave this establishment tonight.'

'Why didn't you go into the township and report it to them?'

'It's miles away. You think I'm going to risk my life out in the scrub on a night like this?'

The innkeeper stoked the fire, laying one log on top of another. The sparks flew up the chimney. He poured two tankards. These he sat on the table with a crock of pickled eggs.

'You've had no supper I take it?' The publican asked. Jim shook his head. 'Aye well I won't let it be said that the inn doesn't serve supper to travelers. Eat and drink while you tell me what happened.'

Jim took a deep breath and told his story. 'What's to be done? There's a murderer in the colony roaming about that ought to be strung up.'

'Aye, and is masquerading as one of the king's men,' the innkeeper concluded. 'You have to tell the authorities.'

'What if I get the blame? What if I'm accused of the murder?'

'Do you suggest that you leave a body to rot in that house and keep it all under your hat?' The innkeeper was clear. 'No one but an innocent man reports a murder that he's witnessed. You only look guilty if you try and hush it up. But don't go to the barracks at Wallis Plains. They're a shoddy bunch. Take it straight to Commandant Morisset.'

Nineteen

Emma headed for the parsonage. Mrs. Brown was outside talking to Kevin as he worked in the garden. When she looked up to see Emma, the woman threw her arms up in pleasure.

'It has been too long since you came for tea. Still, you're here now. Where is your aunt? Why did you not bring her to call? I suppose that being in mourning she doesn't like to step out.'

Emma shook her head. 'Aunt Adelaide is not yet well enough. She isn't herself.'

Mrs. Brown surveyed Emma knowingly. 'And nor yet are you, I would imagine.' The parson's wife missed little.

Although Kevin's face lit up to see her, his smile was not what it usually was. Tobias's conviction weighed on them all in different ways. 'How are Mary and Katy?'

'Mary and Katy are well, miss, but they would be a sight happier if Toby was away out of that cell. Still, we live in hope, don't we Mrs. Brown?'

'We do indeed, Kevin.' Mrs. Brown agreed, before she took Emma's hand. 'You are overwrought, my dear. You need a cup of tea and a wedge of treacle tart.'

If tea, sweets and pleasantries could remedy the situation, Emma would have sat down willingly. As it was, Emma began to object. The last thing she felt she could manage was food. Her appetite had abandoned her altogether.

'Don't refuse me, Emma. You look unwell, and even though you may not feel like eating, I insist you do.' She looked at Emma earnestly. 'As a friend who cares,' she added, and led Emma into the manse and sat her down. Emma was overcome with gratitude. She tried to veil her sadness, but the woman saw it all. She sat down beside Emma.

'Do you think I don't know? Aren't you aware my dear that when that strapping big man was dragged to gaol, the townsfolk in the colony watched from every road, cottage gate and window? That you love him is no sin to me. That you were engaged to Officer Quinn and might have made the mistake of marrying him, might have been.'

Emma looked up at the woman in surprise and was given a wink.

'Chin up. I have a wonderful idea, but I won't tell you and we won't budge from this house until I see food pass your lips.'

'Your advice is sound, because it comes from the heart.'

'So you must do as you are bid,' Mrs. Brown smiled, coming back to the table with a generous slice of tart on each plate.

'Now, I know what's being bandied around the town. I am aware of what that young man of yours is accused of, and I tell you right now, I don't believe a word of it. He worked for us you will remember, in the place Kevin now holds, and there was nothing but honesty and goodness in Tobias. He needs his friends to hold strong together in support until his innocence is proven. Eat up and I'll tell you what we're going to do.'

Emma looked in consternation at the tart, and then made a start. It was actually very good. She hadn't noticed how weak and listless she had become until now. The wall of strength she had tried to erect began to crumble like tart pastry. Now, under the ministration of a caring friend, Emma swallowed on the lump in her throat.

'I have simmered a cauldron of mutton broth. It's far too much for us, and I suggest we take some to that overgrown Irishman of yours. Not only that, but it's baking day today, and I think it would be very nice to share my kitchen with you, Emma. We will not only take him a basin of soup, but something filling from the girdle. Scones perhaps? We have no jam, but we can sweeten them with a good amount of sugar. They do just as nicely buttered, don't you think?'

'Tobias will be grateful,' Emma was close to tears.

'Now wait while I find you an apron, dear. You don't want to go and see Tobias covered in flour, now do you?'

The two women enjoyed the hours together. Emma even found herself laughing at some small anecdote shared by the parson's wife. Had Mrs. Brown ever thought to take in a lodger? But then, Emma had no money with which to pay board in any case.

'Will you come with me to visit Tobias?'

'I will walk the road with you, Emma dear, but you must face the rest yourself. That you man wants to see you more than anything right now, I'd say, and you're going to give him just that. Only make sure you tell Tobias that I showed you how to cook drop scones,' she chuckled.

'The idea was all yours, and a good one at that. The last weeks have been difficult, and I have had a lovely morning. Thank you for your kindness.'

'What good are friends for if they are only around to share the easy times? It's during the hardest moments when we need friends the most.' Mrs. Brown took Emma by the arm to waylay her.

'Tell Tobias I will see him when he returns.'

Emma swallowed. What if Tobias never returned? What if the worst happened? Mrs. Brown must have seen Emma's doubt.

'I will think of nothing but his imminent release,' the woman told her, stopping at the end of their street to wave Emma goodbye. Mrs. Brown was determined to believe, to trust, even when all seemed hopeless.

She left the parson's wife with a smile still on her face. When she entered the gaol, the smile slipped and fell. Emma cleared her throat and spoke tentatively.

'I've come to see Tobias Freeman.' The gaoler looked her

over slowly.

'What have you got in the basket?' He ignored the request but not the aroma that wafted from beneath the tea cloth.

'I have food for Tobias Freeman,' she flushed.

He considered. He looked as thought he might well refuse her.

'You can leave them on the counter here if you want to. I can take them to him.'

She guessed that his intentions were far from noble. 'I would prefer to give them to him myself.'

He nodded grudgingly before leaving his chair to pick up the circle of keys hanging on the wall. He passed her without a word and Emma followed him.

The nauseating odour of the open-air midden beside the hospital was woeful, but Emma found that the gaol was little better. The reek of stale sweat and night soil was almost tangible. She resisted the urge to put a hand over her mouth, and put out a hand to find her bearings instead, because the gaol appeared as black as the Newcastle coal seam itself. She held a basket in one hand as she felt her way with the other. Walking into the unknown, she shivered.

'Your heart is here; first cell on the right.'

The commandant had said so. How right he had been. Her pity and sadness for Tobias were so great that she almost wanted to turn back and walk out into the sunshine, so that he didn't have her witness his shame. Yet her visit might be the only ray of warmth he felt that day, and it was this that kept her feet moving forward. Her eyes adjusted to the dimness and she tried not to dwell on the stench.

The turnkey unlocked the door.

'Wakey wakey, rise and shine. What, still abed at noon? For shame, sir I do hope you had a shave!'

Emma couldn't bear to hear any more. 'That will be all,

thank you,' she told the soldier pointedly.

The sardonic smile was replaced with an even less palatable look. Still, it had the desired effect. 'Call out when you are ready.'

Emma walked into the cell and set down the basket.

Tobias stood waiting, arms at his side. He was hardly visible, and only then for the mercy of a small claustrophobic window at the very top of the far wall. When he put his arms out to draw her in, Emma fell willingly into his embrace. She pulled away to look at him. She took in the swelling on his face, and guessed that he would probably have given as good as he got. Yet fights were never fair if it was not man to man.

'They beat you.' It was not a question.

'Aye, well they tried,' he smiled a little. 'I gave them something to remember me by.'

She put up a hand to touch the black stubble on his jaw; the ruggedly handsome face. Tobias covered her hand with his own.

Before she left she would see that he ate the contents of the basket, because even in the poorly lit room, she could tell that he had not been given adequate rations. Emma felt tears well. She willed them away.

She made a valiant bid at small talk. Told him of the morning that she had spent with Mrs. Brown, and that Kevin had sent his fondest regards.

'How is your aunt? Your uncle?' He asked.

Emma bit her lip. 'My aunt has given me an ultimatum.'

'What about?' Tobias frowned.

'Your life is more pressing than my comfort,' Emma assured him, brushing aside his look of dismay.

Tobias grabbed her hands and sat down with her on the straw mattress on the floor.

'If relations grow worse, I want you to go to the boarding

house and tell mistress McGuiness you are to take my room.'

Emma frowned and opened her mouth to speak.

'Emma, please just listen to me. There is well over twenty-three pounds, and if worst comes to worst ... '

'No, please don't say it. I won't hear it ... ' She covered her ears, and he pulled them away, held them firmly within his own.

His voice was raw, deep and dreadful. 'Sometimes fate deals a heavy hand.'

'Would you will your life away so easily, Tobias?' She heard her voice break.

'No,' he vowed, 'never, but if the very worst happens, you will have the money behind you. You will have something to see you through. The money from my pardon was to be for our future. If I am condemned, all I have is for you alone. Do you hear me? Either to continue life here, or to take you back home. I want you to go to the landlady, tell her that you have considered boarding with her, and that you will continue to rent my room. Under the bed there is a floorboard with a knot like angels wings. You will be able to loosen it, and that's where you'll find the money. Will you do it, Emma?' he pleaded. 'Will you do that for me?' Emma nodded, saddened to her very soul.

'Yes, Tobias my love, I will.'

'I want you to do it directly. I need to know that you're all right. That's all I need.'

'Now, will you do something for me?' Emma asked caressing him, his cheeks, his forehead, his hair.

'Aye, of course I will. For you, anything,' his assurance was absolute.

Emma got up from the ticking and lifted the basket. 'Eat everything I put on your plate.'

'Aye, Ma, I will.' He sat up straight as a schoolboy, waiting with a grin. Tobias and Emma made to laugh, but Emma choked on the awful prospect of the noose.

She wept in the circle of his arms.

Twenty

The tribe had gone hunting. Gideon hadn't cared to join them. He was content for them to set food down before him without having to move off the skins to help kill for meat, and for quite a while, hadn't been physically capable of it, even if he'd wanted to.

He had been with them for a long time now, he supposed, but then one day was just like another. He had nowhere he needed to go, and nothing he needed to do, and so he would lay back yawning as he watched their day-to-day activities. But as his strength had returned, his mind had begun to question all the things he needed answers for.

Gideon stood near the porch of his house. Native grasses grew long where the lawn sloped down to the river. He blinked slowly, looking at the reeds in vague recollection. He remembered a scuffle with some ruffian down by the bank. He recalled searing pain.

Then there were memories of flies and hard ground and lying beside the camp fire. The sound of the blacks as they talked together while he dozed, with no more understanding of their words than he comprehended the song of crickets after dusk.

He felt his face with tentative fingertips. It was still sensitive. Still sore. His fingers traced his sightless eye. When he had been inside the house, he had seen for himself in the looking glass that he was different. It didn't bother him, with the exception of the dull ache that continued to niggle. He had looked at one side of his face, and then the other, and he tried to remember his life before. Some of it had returned to him, but the rest was like a series of fragmented dreams.

He recalled the painted harlot in the upstairs room. He hadn't stopped to ask what she was doing in his house, he just knew that she was intruding where he and Emma were supposed to live. She had been just another titivated woman.

He thought back to early days, when his mother had painted the streets of London. The night one of her callers had tied a cravat around her neck to throttle the life from her. If the door hadn't been open, the man might well have fulfilled his intention, but at twelve years old, Gideon had pulled the man from her, striking a stunning blow to his head with an iron doorstop.

Gideon had turned away at his mother's unashamed nakedness. He had been so angry with her for shaming him, for shaming herself. He had flushed fiercely, turning away as he considered how to get rid of the scoundrel. With his mother's help, he had dragged the body to the river. The water had received the body with a forgetful sigh to float along the Thames. His mother later told him that he had met his father.

The introduction had been the first and the last.

He frowned, trying to remember still more. He knew the house at his back was his. He also knew that Emma ought to have been there. Yet in the place of chaste Emma had been some harpy cavorting as if for some male audience, laughing at unheard jokes, smiling and speaking to some imaginary gentleman in dulcet tones. Any flame of charity had been extinguished as he watched her pitiful show. He had felt no more remorse for her demise than he had for the girl he remembered fawning by the dock.

He blinked, looking up at the sightless eyes of the house. He wondered where Emma was, and why she wasn't at home. She was never here when he arrived, and there was nothing in the house to eat.

Although she kept him warm at night, he didn't care for the gin. The natives didn't like him and now he had to snatch at meat from their fires if he wanted to fill his belly.

✠

Emma looked up at her aunt. She hadn't heard a word the woman had said. Aunt Adelaide's look of disdain was like a cast off gown. Emma had not grown used to it, but she wore it. Let it fall over her shoulders. It weighed her down.

Emma had to forgive her aunt on a daily basis, because bitterness was too easy a current to drown in. Forgiveness took more fortitude. Emma knew her aunt wanted none of it. She scorned Emma's every gesture of charity.

'I'm sorry, Aunt Adelaide. I didn't hear what you said.'

The apology met with a resentful look. Emma made an effort to counter it with understanding.

'Your mind is occupied elsewhere.' It was an accusation, but it was nothing more than the truth. Emma didn't try to deny it.

'I *said* that I am going to begin on some handwork for Phoebe's arrival.' Emma hoped that the '*arrival*' would help to salve some of the pain of Euphemie's passing.

'I have begun on the same,' Emma said. Her hands had been employed on welcoming gifts for Phoebe's babe, but in truth her heart had been with Tobias, stitching him deeper into the fabric of her heart.

'I am glad to hear that you have put your mind to something more than the felon we were foolish enough to welcome into our home.' Aunt Adelaide went on, 'You know what I told you regarding your loyalty?'

'I do,' Emma nodded, preparing for her aunt's words.

'I stick to what I said. I know you've been visiting him again. I know you took him food, even though he is fed well enough in gaol. Our burden is hard enough, without your disloyalty pulling harder on the yoke.'

Emma stood, straightened her shoulders, shrugging off the burden of her aunt's dislike. She would not wear it anymore.

'You don't have to ask me, Aunt Adelaide. I'll leave of my

own free will, just as I came. I thank you for your hospitality towards me. I'm only sorry that you understand your own hurt so well, but that you can't feel the suffering of others. I apologise if I have caused you more grief. It was never my intention.'

'I will tell your uncle when he comes home from the hospice this evening that you need some space. I'll make sure he understands.'

Scalding tears spilled over Emma's cheeks. She would make her farewell to her uncle herself. She wasn't altogether sure that he saw things in the same way her aunt did, but lately he was long-suffering and forgave her aunt much.

Being unwanted was one of the hardest things that Emma had ever had to bear. With straight back and a still tongue, Emma went to the bedroom she had once shared with Phoebe and Euphemie, and got her things together. As to her heavy trunk, that was a hurdle she would have to find a way to jump some other time.

Emma left the silent cottage. Aunt Adelaide was nowhere to be seen. This might have been deliberate, yet it saved them both being uncomfortable. Emma wasn't sure if she was supposed to say her goodbyes or not, if they were expected or even wanted. A hard task indeed not to resent Aunt Adelaide as much as she found herself resented.

Emma met her uncle walking towards home. He was frail and thin but he carried a cheerful smile. For an instant he had the look of her father. He had been a clergyman, yet both men had professions with a duty of care. Emma swallowed down her emotions as he limped towards her.

'Emma dear, you're lucky to catch me. You must have known I was to come home early today.' He went to take her arm for their walk back to the cottage, as was their wont. Emma stopped him with a hand, gentle upon his arm while she explained.

'But Emma, you can't,' he argued. 'Your home is with us. You suffer over Tobias, and you need people around you to love and support you, as we all do.'

'Aunt Adelaide is of a different opinion. She doesn't see it the way you do.'

'I know.' He hung his head and shouldered the guilt as though the fault was his own.

'I don't blame you, Uncle George, and I don't blame Aunt Adelaide. There's no point making things worse for any of us.'

'These are hard times for the whole family, my dear. We must stay firm in faith for brighter days ahead.' There were tears in his eyes. 'Don't leave, Emma.' She saw the suffering there. It must have felt as though everyone was leaving him.

'I'll be there to roll bandages at the hospital tomorrow morning,' Emma assured him on a bright smile. 'I'm not going anywhere.'

'Where on earth will you stay?' he asked, barely registering her attempt at humour.

'Mistress McGuiness's boarding house.'

He shook his head sadly. 'With what means?'

'With Tobias's reward that he was given for capturing Max Metcalfe.'

'You might have been dead to us if Tobias hadn't rescued you from that villain.'

'Aunt Adelaide did tell me that bushrangers lurk where you least suspect. She had been correct.' Emma's smile was rueful.

'This is a very sad state of affairs. You know, I love my wife Adelaide, but I am the head of the household, and I tell you that if you will come back with me, I will welcome you to our house with open arms.'

'I know, Uncle George. I'll remember it with gratitude; always.' She said, 'Tobias's trial is in two days.'

'I will be there. Never fear. Not everyone gives any credit to the tongues of gossips. I for one will be there as a friend, and as your family,' he told her firmly.

'We will sit together,' Emma whispered, close to tears.

'Indeed we will.' Emma walked the last steps to the boarding house of Mistress McGuiness.

The front door was open to welcome lodgers. Emma pulled the bell and waited.

She met the woman with a smile.

It was returned with curiosity if not cordiality.

'Good afternoon, Mistress McGuiness, I would like to enquire about lodgings.'

'I have a room available.'

'I want one room in particular.'

'Aye?' The landlady cocked her head.

'I would like the room that Mr. Tobias Freeman has been staying in.' The owner of the boarding house looked askance.

'You can't have that room. Mr. Freeman's things are in there.'

'I have been given permission by him to lodge in that room, and oversee his personal effects.'

Mistress McGuiness put her hands on her hips. 'Well, he didn't mention it to me.'

Emma took a deep breath.

'I understand that, but circumstances don't permit for him to be able to consult you.'

'Then I'm afraid you cannot have the room.'

'If you cannot take my word as true, then I will go and ask Commandant Morisset to come and explain the nature of my friendship with Mr. Freeman to you.' Emma flushed even as she whispered the words.

'The nature of your relationship with that man is no secret to anyone. Still, there's no need to bother the commandant.

Please come in.'

Emma barely regarded what Mistress McGuiness told her concerning times for supper and breakfast. As she followed her up the stairs, Emma ruminated on what Tobias had told her.

'*Under the bed there is a floorboard with a knot like angels wings.*'

She hoped she would be able to find what she was looking for.

When the woman opened the door, Emma put a hand out to support herself. Here was his jacket hanging over the chair. There was his cravat folded neatly on the bed. The Bible she had given him rested on the pillow. Emma turned to her hostess to dismiss her with cursory thanks, but she was unable to speak for emotion.

'I'll see you in the dining room for supper. I'll be serving a saddle of mutton and suet pudding.'

If only all the broken hearts in the world could be helped by a hearty supper and pudding to follow.

Emma closed and locked the door behind herself. She caressed the bedspread as though it was Tobias that her hands rested upon. Then, getting down upon her hands and knees, she found the floorboard that Tobias had told her about. It wasn't easy to dislodge, but when she accomplished it, she smiled, for there in the recess she found a wealth of holey dollars and dumps the like of which she had never seen.

But it was the small velvet pouch that next took her attention, and she plucked it from the coins to see what her love might have kept inside.

It was a ring of gold, new and gleaming, made for a woman's finger. It shone in the palm of Emma's hand. Now she understood what had taken him to Sydney. Returning it to the little pouch, Emma tucked it reverently back where it had come from. She curled up on Tobias's bed with the Bible that had been given to her before the voyage to New South Wales. On the flyleaf it read:

> *Courage sister,*
> *Do not stumble,*
> *Though thy path be black as night,*
> *There's a star to guide the humble,*
> *Trust in God and do the right.*

A butcher bird perched on the sill. It seemed as though it wore a black hooded cape. An executioner's mask of sorts. An image of Tobias covered by the hood of a man condemned came unbidden and unwanted, and she wondered how much darker the days would get.

Twenty-one

Tobias was escorted into the courthouse. He was confronted by a curious flock. Eagerly craned necks; townsfolk with bold eyes and long stares. Seats filled with people who had come for the entertainment. Tobias was supported by a meagre clutch of friends. Aye, he could count them on one hand, but they were there. When he took the stand to swear an oath, the first glance he met was Emma's.

Her face was pale and wan, but she smiled as though the sun shone just to see him. The joy in seeing her was bitter-sweet.

He had grown haggard since his time in the gaol. With an unkempt beard and unwashed skin, he smelled of stale washing and sweaty stockings. The claret cravat had been put aside, for he was a ticket of leave gentleman no more. He bowed his head and hoped that Emma hadn't smelled the taint of him as he passed.

His journey since leaving Ireland had been a long one. From convict chains to emancipation, then back to gaol again, his journey to redemption was not yet over. But he didn't want to be redeemed in death, like some martyr. He wanted to be absolved from this crime because he was an innocent man. He would not walk to the noose without protest.

But all the same his hands shook and his innards quaked, and when he was made to sit he was grateful, for he thought he might just fall.

'I am a guest from Sydney, and like Commandant Morisset, I was also a magistrate until I retired from my post. The commandant has graciously asked me to lead this trial. So with that brief introduction, let us begin.' He peered at Tobias from beneath his brows. 'Do you know why you are here, Mr. Freeman?'

'No, I do not.'

The audience tittered. The judge's eyebrows rose to his wig like a bemused koala waking from a nap. The judge was going to play the crowd. Tobias wasn't duped.

'Well, that's very remiss of the constabulary, is it not?'

Tobias made no reply, knowing the man wanted to show him as a fool, to belittle and shake him. He ignored it. It was the only card he had to play.

The judge waited, but when he saw that Tobias was not going to reply further he said, 'I will enlighten you then, Mr. Tobias Freeman, on why you are before the colony today. It is simply this: you have been charged of a heinous crime. Do you know the nature of this crime that I speak, sir?'

'No, I don't.'

The judge chuckled and invited the crowd to take his lead. This they were more than happy to do. He let them snicker for a moment before he went on.

'The crime I speak of is murder, and you have been named as the perpetrator.' The judge punctuated the effect of his words with a moment's silence.

'Two women, innocent ladies without the strength to defend themselves, were brutally strangled. And you, upon both occasions, were the one to see them last.' The crowd made a noise of hushed horror. The ringleader, for this is what he was, worked the gallery with his every gesture and nuance. He nodded towards the audience, shaking a solemn finger. It was like a puppet show. 'You are a big man, are you not, Mr. Freeman?'

'Aye, Your Honour,' Tobias admitted readily. There was no lie in that.

'How tall would you say you are?' The judge weighed him up speculatively.

'I don't know,' Tobias shrugged. 'I know I look down on everyone I talk to.' He cringed at the pun. Realised how foolish the words made him sound. It didn't escape the judge. He smiled condescendingly. The crowd guffawed.

'Did you look down on Cecily Quinn and the surgeon's daughter, Miss Euphemie?' This was quietly asked.

'No,' Tobias answered, meeting the eye of the judge, 'I did not.'

The judge made a placating motion, as though he didn't want to rile Tobias. There was no need for the action, and they both knew it. Tobias took a deep breath. Let it out as steadily as he was able.

'Would you mind stepping over to the wall sir, so that the constable here might give us more than an estimation of your height?'

Tobias stood to do as he was bid, the chains on his ankles dragging heavily in the courthouse. A ponderous sound, and well-remembered. The sound knotted his stomach.

Tobias heard the judge exclaim. 'My, oh my, a tall man indeed, ladies and gentlemen. Mr. Tobias Freeman is approximately six feet and five inches tall. I must admit sir, standing beside you I feel quite defenceless.'

Tobias said nothing. The judge was out to tar and feather him. It didn't take a fool to see that. Tobias was bid sit. He lumbered to his seat.

'With such height doubtless comes great strength. You are a strong man, are you not, Mr. Freeman?'

'Aye Your Honour, I suppose I am. But then any man is strong in comparison to a woman. It doesn't make me a brute or yet a murderer, for I'm neither.'

'Now, now, Mr. Freeman, I have said no such thing. My words only implicated your strength.'

The man had goaded him, and now Tobias's words made him look if anything, guilty. He bit his lip and tasted blood.

'Will you tell the ladies and gentlemen know what crime

you were accused of in Ireland?'

Tobias sighed. 'Murder.'

The man threw up his hands and the crowd stood and hollered. The judge shook his head sadly. For a space of minutes he let the crowd have its head. They shouted.

They spat and punctuated curses with their fists.

After long moments the judge made a pacifying motion with his hands. The audience sat at his will. Tobias looked around him at the nightmarish charade.

'It was an accident!' Tobias cried.

The judge nodded. 'It always is.'

Tobias was desperate to explain. 'The man defiled my sister. I knocked him down and he hit his head on the hearth. It killed him. He was a so-called gentleman farmer whose family had sway in the county. I was convicted when I should have been thanked. That man was a terror to every maid that worked on that farm. I may have been the cause of his death, but when that man died, every colleen for miles around was made safe because of it!'

'Colleen, Mr. Freeman? Who on earth is she?'

'I meant every girl, Your Honour,' Tobias said.

'That's more like it Mr. Freeman; you're not in Ireland now, you know.' Tobias flushed. His cheeks burned, the smell of his sweat overripe.

The judge sat back, crossing his hands over his paunch. 'Let us ascertain the reason for your journey down the Hunter River with Mistress Quinn. Why did you take her there?'

'She asked me if I would ferry her to Wallis Plains so that she could see the grave of her son, Officer Gideon Quinn.'

'Why you?'

'I was the one she asked. There seemed to be no one else who would do it.'

'She paid you handsomely?' The judge asked. Tobias shook his head.

'No, your Honour, she paid me nothing.' Here the judge prompted the crowd with a look of interest.

'Ooh,' the audience made the sound as one.

'Why were you not paid for your services, Mr. Freeman? You must have been sorely disillusioned to have traveled the distance on a promise not met?'

'I wouldn't take the coin.'

'Come, come, Mr. Freeman, do you mean to tell me that you performed the task without want for payment?'

'Aye, Widow Quinn offered me money but I refused. She asked me to stay and work for her, but I told her I would work for no one, but did it as a favour.'

'Why would you do this, sir? Do I sit in the presence of a saint?' The judge chuckled, making light of what Tobias had done.

'No, Your Honour, I'm no angel. I felt sorry for her. She had come from London to find her son, only to be told that he had died. She was disappointed that I wouldn't stay on.' Tobias shrugged. 'It was the least I could do.'

'For the information of ladies and gentlemen here, Widow Quinn was found by a peddler and his wife shortly after the event. We know this because in the morning when they found her, there was no decomposition of the body evident, and the stub of a candle still burned within the house. Further evidence showed that the deceased had been throttled with her own hair. The heinous appetites of sick men,' the judge shook his head and went on.

'Now let's go backward in time just a little if we may. Miss Euphemie was to see her sister married. Sadly she never arrived at the church. She had been missing since the previous evening.

It was thought that nobody saw her. But you saw her, did you not, Mr. Freeman? The night wasn't quite so dark as you had hoped,' he said, staring at Tobias long and hard. 'I'd like to invite Mistress McGuiness to the stand if I may.'

Tobias looked up, dumbstruck as the woman made her way to the stand. She would not meet his eye. Mistress McGuiness swore on the Bible and looked steadfastly to the judge.

'What did you see the night before the surgeon's daughter's wedding, Mistress McGuiness? Tell us, as succinctly as you may, what you witnessed.'

'I was readying myself for bed when I realised that I had left the teapot on the step earlier that evening. I had emptied the leaves into the garden and put it down to attend to something else, only to forget to take the pot back inside. So later that night when I went to get it, I heard voices. It was a man and a woman, and I know there's only one Irish giant this side of the Coal River. It was Tobias Freeman, and he was talking to Miss Euphemie. She wanted him to do something but he said he wouldn't do it.'

Aye, you've enough grace to blush, as well you might, Tobias thought.

'Anyway, Your Honour, I crept over towards the gate and I saw her put her hands on him. He wasn't happy about it, and he backed away. I could tell he was angry because of his tone of voice. Then I heard more people speaking. They were coming down the road from the public house, and Mr. Freeman and Miss Euphemie looked up. I was afraid of being seen, so I tiptoed back inside the house.'

The courthouse was deathly silent. And for all that the curious congregation perched cheek by jowl on pews, the place was as cold as the grave to Tobias. For their hearts held no more warmth than charity, and that was precious little.

'Did you take the teapot inside, Mistress McGuiness?' the judge asked. The woman shook her head.

'I forgot. It stayed there until morning.'

The judge looked heavenward and crossed his hands piously. 'Pity it is you didn't go back outside that night, Mistress McGuiness; you might have witnessed the diabolical crime. Better yet, your neighbourly presence might well have prevented it.'

The audience made an appreciative noise in agreement. 'That will be all. Thank you Mistress McGuiness.' Then the judge addressed the men and women in the court.

'I'd like to point out to you, ladies and gentlemen, that Miss Euphemie met her end in exactly the same way as Mistress Quinn. I'd further like to remind you that Tobias Freeman was the last person known to see both women alive.'

'I would ask you to search back over what you've been told this day, and you will recall that Tobias Freeman was a convicted felon, charged by the crown for an act of violence which ended in murder.'

The crowd got to their feet and yelled in outrage. The judge held up his hands as though he were balancing the scales of justice. Tobias had never seen such a conjurer in all his days. The man could have made his living on the stage.

Tobias saw the commandant out of the corner of his eye as he made his way towards the judge. He stopped to speak in confidence to him before he took the stand.

'Although this is irregular, Commandant Morisset would like to say a few words regarding Mr. Freeman. You may swear your oath, then you may go ahead.'

'Firstly I would like to speak regarding the character of this man here on trial.' The commandant gestured at Tobias, then looked back to the crowd. 'I know for a fact that he recently helped to save the life of a little girl in the colony, without thought of his own welfare, even though he knew his act might have seen him flogged. I was there when he brought in bushranger Max Metcalfe, a felon who had evaded capture for some time. He had the opportunity to head bush himself with the criminal, but instead he plied the barge from Wallis Plains to Newcastle, without ever knowing that there was a pardon and a twenty-five dollar reward.'

'Singular behaviour,' the judge was thoughtful. 'Surely he did know, Commandant Morisset, for why else would a convict do such a deed?'

'It is become a sad world indeed, Your Honour, if a man cannot do what is right, without suspicion as to the motive.'

The judge's brows lowered over his eyes.

'Do you forget that the man in question is charged with murder?' The judge asked.

'I don't forget it for a minute, Your Honour, and I can tell you that Tobias Freeman was not necessarily the last person to see Miss Euphemie before she died.' Here he paused and looked at the crowd.

'I had been playing cards with numerous gentlemen. Mr. Freeman was in the establishment too. He left just before me. Doubtless he spoke to Miss Euphemie, but so did I, because she was waiting for me near the boarding house owned by Mistress McGuiness.' The commandant paused, as thought to choose his words carefully.

'Miss Euphemie had made her interest towards me plain enough on more than one occasion. This night she spoke to Mr. Freeman to ask that he talk me around in her favour. I know this because she told me. She was displeased because he said he wouldn't do it. Miss Euphemie wasn't happy that Tobias, or rather, Mr. Freeman wouldn't do her bidding. The way she saw it, even though he had been given his freedom, he was still a convict. I told her as gently as I could that I had no interest in her beyond that of a friendly acquaintance. My only mistake was that I walked away. I know now that I ought to have walked her home.'

The commandant nodded towards the magistrate, left the stand and sat down, to noises of dismay and regret from the audience.

'Thank you for your candour, Commandant Morisset. The audience appreciates your honest testimony. However, the murders of these two women are too similar to be ignored, and both these crimes see Mr. Freeman in the picture.'

'Perhaps, Mr. Freeman, you were angry because the young woman saw you as a convict, an indentured man. Perhaps it made you see red that Cecily Quinn expected you to toil for her when you stated to us quite firmly that nothing would induce you to work for any man? Perhaps the lashes on your back have scarred you in ways that the eye cannot see ... Perhaps, Mr. Freeman, you are guilty as charged.'

Twenty-two

The publican had talked him into it. A few stiff drinks and a fatherly arm around his shoulders had helped Jim make a wise decision. So the innkeeper had said. Now the horse was hitched and Jim stood outside Tam's doorstop, banging on the cottage door.

Tam traveled with Jim. He was always a stout friend in time of need, and the last thing Jim wanted was to travel alone. The journey to Newcastle would be made shorter for the company. It was a tedious trip made alone when it could be done with two. The faceless redcoat he feared was no spectre, and daylight or no, Jim knew that the fiend could materialise from anywhere. A chilly thought.

'I just hope that I'm not locked up when I tell the authorities what I saw,' Jim mumbled.

'Of course you won't be. Besides, the old girl can't lay and rot in that big house, Jimmy my lad. It would be a sin to leave her like that.'

'Well, I didn't do it.'

'Aye, I ken that well enough, but that headless redcoat has to be found, or no one's safe.'

'He wasn't headless,' Jim told him irritably. 'He had a head. It was a face that he was short of. One side looked like it had melted down his neck like a tallow candle.' Jim shuddered.

'Maybe it was a trick of the light,' Tam sounded like he found the description a little far-fetched.

Jim looked at him darkly. 'Just hope he never looks you in the eye, Tam, because if he does, you'd better be saying your prayers for deliverance.'

'That's why the authorities need to know.'

'You're right, Tam.' Jim chanced a glance in the cart behind them. Of course, there was no one there. Tam looked at him and he saw a new horror overtake Jim.

'What's wrong?' Tam asked, darting a look around them into the scrub.

'Do you remember when I had a load to deliver to Newcastle last summer?'

'Aye.'

Jim shivered as goosebumps raised the hairs on his flesh. 'You remember the accident with the surgeon?'

'It wasn't your fault, any more than the incident with the old lady in the big house,' Tam assured him. 'You weren't used to driving a team, that was all.'

'When the doctor rolled under the cart, I was pretty shaken up. I'd had more than a tipple of rum.'

'But you didn't cause the accident, surely?' Tam asked.

'No, but it wasn't until I was driving the cart out of town that I realised something.'

'Aye?' Tam prompted, giving Jim his full attention.

'That the officer with the surgeon hadn't just seen it happen, but had *made* it happen.' A finger of unease made Jim shudder.

'You were in your cups and might have been mistaken,' Tam suggested. Jim turned, reins in hand, to stare at Tam.

'The redcoat was the same man.'

Tam's jaw dropped. 'So he had no face?'

'There was nothing wrong with his face,' Jim pondered, trying to pinpoint what it was in his memory that struck a chord.

'Then it can't have been him. Was it just because he wore a red coat?' Tam was dubious.

Jim shook his head. 'I stood near him, I spoke to him, cocky little bantam of a fella he was. It was that voice of his, and the colour of his eyes.'

'You're really starting to give me the heebie-jeebies now Jim.

And why are you going around looking into men's eyes?'

'They were pale as a raven's,' Jim recollected the moment. 'And the tuneless whistle as he walked down the road, well, I would never forget it. It just hit me.'

'I don't want to hear any more, Jimmy lad. I don't care to hear about the tone of his voice or the blue of his peepers, whether he rode a horse backwards with his head screwed off and it was on his lap yapping like a ventriloquist's dummy. I just want to get into Newcastle before dark. At this rate, I know I'll end up dying of fright, and that, my lad, will be all your fault.'

So Jim whipped up the pair, his own mare Nancy, and Tam's horse as well. He looked straight ahead with a diligence born of fear. The scrub was thick enough to hide a body that lurked in wait. Let other men dare fate. He was content to be a coward.

'A good feed and a comfortable bed will be in order.' Tam was jovial.

'I wish I had Polly to roll in the blankets with.'

'Marry the lass, Jim, and you can do just that every night of the week.'

'I'd hoped to get a start working for the old lady, but that's out of the question now. A man needs money to begin married life with, and I can't see myself getting wed without a nest egg.'

'Someone will end up taking the house on, and they'll be bound to need yard help,' Tam reasoned. 'You might be lucky yet.'

They came to the Broad Meadow and Jim breathed a sigh. In next to no time they would be rumbling through the streets of the colony. It wouldn't be a moment too soon.

Supper and slumber came just as Tam promised. But when Jim and Tam went to seek out the commandant the next morning, they were told that he wasn't available.

'I don't know when he'll return,' the officer told them. 'He's at a trial at present. If you come back this afternoon, the verdict will have been reached. Doubtless he'll be free to talk to you then.' Jim looked at the officer and wondered whether to tell him his tale.

'It's about an old woman who was murdered in Wallis Plains,' Jim began, glancing at Tam for moral support.

'Jim was a witness to the murderer leaving the house,' Tam agreed. The officer looked up, frowning.

'Is that so?'

Jim nodded, warming to his story but not to the steely-eyed officer. He had the soldier's attention now though, that was sure.

'I wanted to tell the commandant that the killer is walking around Wallis Plains and needs to be locked up.'

'Oh no,' the officer assured them with a smile. 'The man will be strung up.'

'Aye, and the devil is disguised as a redcoat, no less.'

Jim nodded the truth of the statement.

The officer frowned. 'You say the man is a soldier of the crown? I find that hard to believe.' The man looked at it as a personal affront.

'I think so. It looked like a redcoat's jacket to me.'

'But any man could don a scarlet coat, could he not?'

'I suppose so,' Jim agreed.

'When the commandant returns you will be able to offer him your information. If you like, I can tell him you dropped in.' The officer even gave them a smile.

Jim and Tam nodded. They told him their names. Jim reached out to shake the officer's hand. The redcoat put his hand out in a half-hearted fashion.

'Officer Octavius Gray.'

Jim left the barracks with Tam, no better off than when they had walked in. 'Think he'll remember to tell the commandant?' Jim asked.

Tam shrugged. 'He didn't act like it was very important.

Didn't even say he'd have someone go to bury the old girl.'

'Feel like we've come here on a wild goose chase. I suppose we'll have to wait around until the trial's over, and go back and see if the commandant's free this afternoon.'

'Aye, I suppose so,' Tam yawned. 'Since we've nothing else to do, we may as well go and see who's on trial. You never know, we might get to speak to the commandant a mite sooner.'

Jim and Tam sat beside a Scotswoman. She smiled to hear a fellow countryman's voice.

'Tobias Freeman is on trial.'

'What's he done?' Tam whispered. A few people sitting on chairs in front turned to scowl. Tam lowered his voice and tried again. 'What's he done?'

'Murder,' the woman shared. 'Strangled the life out of an elderly woman alone in a house at Wallis Plains, her and a young girl here in the town.'

'When did this happen?' Jim and Tam strained to hear her words over that of the judge.

'Just the other day a peddler and his wife went into the house and found that she'd been murdered, not far from the Wheatsheaf Arms. Throttled her with her own hair, he did.'

Jim and Tam stared at one another, then at the giant of a man about to be condemned. Jim heard the words of the judge, as clear and cold as a bell.

'Tobias Freeman, you have been found guilty as charged. You will hang by the neck until you are dead. Do you have anything to say?'

Jim saw the condemned man open his mouth to speak and Jim stood up and called out, 'He's innocent! He'll tell you that, and I will too!' All eyes in the court turned as one. Jim felt the stares of everyone upon him, including the stern face of the judge.

'The sentence has been passed,' the judge said, fixing an eye on Jim, 'and you are in contempt of court.'

'You can't hang an innocent man!' Jim cried, walking up the aisle.

The crowd stood in a wave and the judge hollered, 'Order! There will be order in my court!'

Jim felt his heart begin to hammer, but walked resolutely towards the judge.

There was no going back.

'I want to take the stand,' Jim heard himself say. There was a woman's desperate sob. He glanced to his right to see a lovely dark-haired woman, tears rolling down her cheeks. An elderly man wearing glasses sitting beside her, took and squeezed her hand. Jim blinked in vague recognition but couldn't think where he'd seen the man before.

An officer with dark curling hair and a scar across his face stood and spoke briefly to the judge. The grizzled judge nodded reluctantly and motioned for Jim to do as he would.

'Do you swear the whole truth and nothing but the truth, so help you God?'

'I do,' Jim nodded.

'Then continue, sir, for you have the whole court eating out of the palm of your hand. Careful of your oath, mind, lest the tables are turned.'

'The peddler and his wife may have been at the big house, but it was me who was there when she was murdered.' Jim hesitated and took a steadying breath, and began the grisly tale.

'A search party is all that stands in the way of truth, and I tell you now, Your Honour that the murderer stalks Wallis Plains. An evil killer with a face half eaten in like the core of a rotten wind-fell.'

'A withered winter apple? I cannot take the evidence of just one man,' the judge was dismissive.

The commandant planted his feet and spoke from where he

stood. 'For all the colony knows, I may well have been the last to see Miss Euphemie alive, Your Honour. Will you convict me for the crime of murder, too?'

The judge blinked. Worked his jaws a moment so that his jowls wobbled. Then he turned to the big prisoner and said, 'At present, it seems that you are a free man. I would ask that you do not leave the colony until the killer is found. In the meantime, what do you intend to do?'

'I'm going to go and get myself married, Your Honour.'

Jim saw that the Irish giant had the judge gob-smacked just as surely as if he'd stunned the man with a fist.

Twenty-three

Commandant Morisset stood outside the courthouse. A strategy needed to be put in place, for there was a way to catch this murderer, he was sure.

'As far as I'm concerned, it's all lies.'

He started at the voice, and turned to see the surgeon's wife. 'You don't believe the witness?' Commandant Morisset addressed her.

'Not for a minute,' the woman cried, defending her daughter's honour, where it had been denied the girl at her death.

'What motive would the man have to lie?' The commandant asked. She snorted, derisive.

'A sum of money, I wouldn't doubt.'

The commandant raised a brow, curiosity haggling with incredulity.

'Are you saying that Tobias Freeman paid the witness to buy himself an alibi?'

'I don't know what you refer to when you speak of lullabies, but I can tell you this, Commandant Morisset: there's a recently freed Irish convict in these parts, and the only tune he deserves to hear is the song of the noose swinging in the sea breeze.'

'Every man is innocent until proven to the contrary, madam.'

'Guilty as charged.'

'Charged, my dear lady, not condemned,' the commandant reminded her gently.

'Not yet,' she raised a threatening finger.

She walked away, then turned back as if she'd forgotten something. If it was her husband she'd misplaced, he emerged moments later as though he'd heard her summons. Hurrying after his wife on a rolling limp, he made a bid to catch up to her.

The commandant watched the progress of the surgeon and his wife. Two lost souls, walking towards the brow of the hill; hop-gaited, harbouring grief.

Rory Ferguson came to stand beside him.

'I take it you preferred your wife to stay at home?' the commandant asked him.

'I didn't want her to come to the trial,' Ferguson agreed. 'She's delicate right now.'

'That was wise.'

'Oh, Lordy,' Rory Ferguson groaned. 'Looks like the mother-in-law is stopping by our house.'

The commandant couldn't help but smile.

'For better or worse, Lieutenant Ferguson,' the commandant reminded him.

'Aye, but no one told me that when I tied the knot with Phoebe, I'd have to take on her mother as well.'

'It's called marrying into the family, don't you know?'

'I do now,' the lieutenant admitted with a wry smile.

Commandant Morisset clapped the young man good-heartedly on the back.

'In all seriousness, sir, I think the old girl's not too far short of losing her marbles.'

'Perhaps when that baby of yours chooses to announce itself, it will be the best remedy you could hope for.'

'You might be right,' Rory Ferguson brightened at the prospect. Whether it was for a bouncing baby or a serene mother-in-law, the commandant wasn't sure which.

'Still, that's not for some time yet.'

Rory Ferguson flushed scarlet and the commandant laughed. 'A mite sooner than was planned?'

'Aye,' and then, 'perhaps you'd like to come and share a pot of tea, sir?' He was hopeful, the commandant could see.

'Lieutenant you and I get on. You could say we see eye to eye as it were, so you will doubtless understand when I tell you that I've already taken the time of day with your dear wife's mother, and that is more than enough for the rest of the calendar month.'

'Aye, she's a scary one,' Rory nodded glumly. 'Baby will probably be too afraid to make itself known.'

The commandant guffawed. 'Ferguson, if the child is well past the due date, you will be certain to know the reason why.'

The commandant watched as Rory Ferguson took his leave. All jokes aside, he didn't blame the young man one iota for his reticence with his new mother. It was a sad affair, and the commandant was all the more keen to find the killer of the surgeon's daughter, no matter the manpower it took.

It would be the second time a search party had gone out in the colony and its surrounds. Last time it was to search for the dead; this time it was to look for the living. Every last soldier was accounted for. But if they couldn't find the individual responsible for the crime, what became of Tobias Freeman? How long could he escape the noose? Someone was culpable for the act. Someone would have to pay.

Tobias Freeman was living on borrowed time, regardless of the fact that he wanted to set himself up as a married man. If there was call for a retrial, Tobias Freeman might well swing, with a young woman left as a widow.

He heard a familiar voice, and turned to see Miss Emma Colchester come out of the courthouse. Beside her was Tobias Freeman. The couple received a few pointed looks. His own opinion was that the young lady had probably been in mourning for Quinn long enough. The surgeon's daughter—Miss Euphemie as he knew to refer to her—had been Miss Colchester's cousin and it was reasonable that the young lady should continue her mourning dress at present, but it didn't preclude her tying the knot with Freeman, should she wish.

He caught the outraged stare of Mistress McGuinness, inwardly shook his head, then turned to the young lady.

'Good afternoon, commandant,' Miss Colchester said. He took her hand briefly and bowed.

'Doubtless it has been a long day for you, Miss Colchester, not to mention for you, Mr. Freeman.'

'Aye the morning was pretty glum, but it's shaping for a better afternoon. I'll be seeing tomorrow in a brighter light, that's certain.'

'Now we just need to find the real perpetrator of the crimes.'

'I'll be there to help every step of the way,' the Irishman told him, looking him squarely in the eye. 'If the murderer has a face half as bad as the witness says, then he can't hide forever. God help him when he's found.'

'God cannot save the damned; not in this lifetime.'

Parson Brown and his wife met the group on the courthouse steps, congratulated Tobias, and then went on to exchange pleasantries.

'Where will you stay, Tobias?' Mrs. Brown wanted to know.

'Not in the lockup, I can tell you that much,' Tobias assured her with a smile.

'You can't go back and board with mistress McGuiness.' The lady shook her head and confided, 'I hope the woman has ruined custom for herself.'

'Now, dear,' her husband remonstrated, 'she probably thought she was seeing justice served.' It was a gentle reminder. Mrs. Brown nodded reluctantly.

'I don't blame her for the witness she gave, but a man has pride, and I won't be giving out any more holey dollars to Mistress McGuiness's boarding house. Nor will this young lady beside me,' Tobias said.

'But Miss Colchester is staying with her uncle and aunt, is she not?' The commandant frowned.

'My aunt suffers her loss heavily, and my presence there was more than she could put up with.'

'It was either them or me,' Tobias shrugged. 'Emma was forced to make the choice. She picked me.'

Mrs. Brown shook her head sadly and took Emma in arm. 'Well, my dear, the rectory is no palace, but there is room for you Emma, and you too Tobias, is there not, Mr. Brown?' she asked her husband.

'Without a doubt of it,' her husband agreed. 'Tobias, the vestry is not spacious, but it will be private, and you're more than welcome to sleep there by night and consider the manse your home by day.'

'I'll work in your garden as well as pay our way,' Tobias told them.

'What, and step on our gardener Kevin's toes?' Mr. Brown chuckled. 'We'd never hear the end of it. And as far as payment goes, Tobias, you can just wash your mouth out with soap. We will get by without talk of money changing hands, I'm sure.'

The small party walked leisurely up Prospect Hill, taking in the warmth of the winter sun.

'If you're all right to go on to the manse with the parson and Mrs. Brown,' Tobias told Emma, 'I'll go along to the boarding house and begin to gather our things.'

'It won't hurt the woman to glimpse me walking past the boarding house with you on the way to the barracks, just in case she thinks to bar the premises from you. Constabulary presence plays a loud enough drum.'

Tobias nodded. 'Thank you, commandant. You know, it's a pity the woman has a tongue with a fork running through the middle of it, because she bakes an excellent steak and oyster pie.'

Twenty-four

Tobias knocked at the boarding house door. Mistress McGuiness was slow to answer, and far from happy when she saw who stood before her. She looked him up and down.

'I'm not here to murder you at the foot of your bed, Mistress McGuiness, never fear.'

She eyed him with distrust. 'You can't stay here I'm afraid.'

'Boarding with you, is easily the last thing on my mind, but I do have personal belongings to collect, as does Miss Colchester. I will relieve you of both.'

'I'm happy to bring them out to you, if you'll wait outside the door.'

Tobias put a steadying hand on the door just short of it closing in his face. It seemed the commandant had been correct.

'Aye, you're kindness itself, Mistress McGuiness but I'd rather come inside and get everything myself, if you'll permit.'

'You can't come inside.'

'You have no worry for your honour, I can assure you, but come inside I will, whether invited or no. Must I get the constabulary?'

'Aye, if you're of a mind to do so!'

'The commandant walked with me here, just now. Maybe he'll think it fitting to put you in the stocks for stealing a gentleman's clobber.'

The widow glanced past him in the direction of the stocks in the square, and closer still, the commandant.

'It'll get hot hunched over in those black gowns you wear, for all that it's winter in this place. Aye, and it'll be boring too, when one hour drags on to the next. Just take my word for it. You'd hate the stocks.'

Widow McGuiness threw wide the door angrily. A draught from the sea followed Tobias in. He took the stairs two at a time, put his hand on the handle of the door that had been his during the stay at the boarding house, but it was locked. Tobias turned to the woman in question. She stood watching him at the bottom of the stairs.

'I hardly think you want me to put a shoulder to the timber?'

He leaned against the door-jamb to wait while the woman got the keys, all the while impatient to be with Emma. The owner of the boarding house neither knew nor cared. But her opinion concerned him not at all.

'There's no need to come in with me,' Tobias told her, unwilling to pull up the floorboard as she looked on. 'I'll not be more than a minute.'

She thought about it for a moment and nodded reluctantly. 'Very well.'

Tobias closed the door after him and locked it for good measure. For a moment he feared that the money would be gone. Yet it gleamed in the recess as he prised up the board. He collected it along with the ring in the velvet pouch. Then, slipping on the jacket that Emma must have neatly folded on the seat of the chair, left the room, passing Mistress McGuiness on the stair.

'Thank you, madam.' He gave a curt nod.

'I'll be sure to bolt my doors this night.'

Tobias stopped at the foot of the stairs and turned to face her. 'Aye, perhaps you'd better but it won't be me you need to fear,' he warned. 'For there's a cunning crook in Newcastle's colony, and he's not too particular in his choice of victim, so have a care.'

The woman's face puckered with a mouthful of venom. Tobias closed the door behind him, but not before he heard her let it out in a gasp of outrage. It was an uncharitable thing to have said, but there were some sweet moments amongst the sour in life, and he savoured it.

Vengeance is Mine, sayeth the Lord.

He recalled the well-timed reminder and grinned all the same. Tobias hastened towards the rectory upon the hill. He had thought that he and Emma would have been married by now. When he had been given twenty-five dollars and an unconditional pardon, he had assumed that matrimony would follow shortly thereafter, but events had cropped up one after another.

In the near distance the bells tolled the end of the working day. Tobias was given a jolt of recollection of his early days in the colony. The bells never failed to unsettle him, months though it had been since he had been a government man. Every time he heard their peal he tensed, straightening his spine, ready to labour. Then he would realise that he had been set free. He reminded himself that he didn't have to be a prisoner of the past. Unless he chose to be.

'Toby, mate!' Kevin cried, coming down the road towards him. There was the toil of honest work on his hands.

'Dirty nails and grubby shirt, Kevin. You're a respectable gardener for parson now. Married to Mary and child on the way, you've landed squarely on your feet.'

'I've few complaints,' Kevin grinned, clasping Tobias to him as a long lost friend.

'It is good to see you Kevin.'

'I was afraid they were going to acquaint you with the noose,' Kevin told him honestly. 'Thought the next time I saw you we might both be wearing a set of angel's wings, only I don't reckon they had a pair big enough to fit you, so they let you off the hook.'

They both laughed and slapped one another on the back.

Emma met him at the gate. He smelled lavender, and had a vivid memory of the day he had picked a bunch for her at the insistence of Mrs. Brown. Little had the woman known then that

Tobias had done it more than willingly.

'Tobias, I'm so glad that you are home.'

'Home is wherever you are.'

Emma rested her cheek against his chest. He held her close, emotion thick in his throat as he looked down at her.

'I didn't see many of your belongings at the boarding house,' he said.

'My trunk is still at my aunt and uncle's cottage. I never thought to mention it.'

'I don't know that I'll receive a welcome smile from your aunt, considering the circumstances of late, but someone has to do it for you.'

'You won't receive a charitable greeting, that's certain, but if you leave it until Uncle George finishes his day at the hospital, you'll be allowed in the door, at any rate.'

'It's nothing compared to some of the hurdles I've had to jump over, Emma love, so take the frown from your face and don't worry for me.' He took her hand before they entered the warmth of the parsonage.

'Tobias Freeman, you won't be sitting down to meat without washing the gaol out of your hair. We've got hot water in a tub and you aren't to emerge until you've washed your troubles off with soap.' Mrs. Brown left him. He dropped his bag, threw off his clothes, and immersed himself in the luxury of bathing.

There was fresh meat for supper. The mutton was roasted and running with gravy. A loaf of bread, heady with wild yeast was cooled and cut in generous chunks, and potatoes that had bubbled in the juices along with the lamb were served with such generosity that Tobias could only stare at the wonder of such a feast as he had never had.

'Aye and who's to say I'm not in heaven?' He spoke to no one in particular, shaking his head.

'Emma and I didn't go to all this trouble for nothing you know. So don't just sit and stare at your plate.' Mrs. Brown winked in Emma's direction.

Tobias grinned, then picking up knife and fork, relished all that was set before him.

'The day started off as the worst of days,' he said thickly. 'I thought maybe my time had come. Yet I have been given reprieve, and you invite us into your house with such goodness ... It's overwhelming.'

For once Mrs. Brown chose to say nothing, but her eyes spoke for her. They shone.

When conversation slowed and eyelids drooped, Tobias wished that he could ask Emma out onto the porch so that he could kiss her goodnight. Her cheeks glowed in the light of the hearth fire. He was so full of thankfulness at the day's turnaround, and so full of love for the young woman who sat opposite him.

'I believe it is time to retire, Mr. Brown,' the parson's wife said. The woman glanced meaningfully at her husband. 'Perhaps you will bring a candle in for me?'

'I certainly shall my dear.'

'Goodnight, Tobias and sweet dreams, Emma dear,' Mrs. Brown said. They bid her a goodnight and the parson told Tobias, 'I will be out shortly and we can go together to the vestry with a candle and blankets.'

But the minutes ticked by and still he had not returned. Tobias stood up and walked to Emma's side. He took her hands and pulled her gently from the chair. Then, wrapping his arms around Emma, Tobias embraced her.

'There's something I want to ask you, Emma, but in all honesty I'm not at liberty to do so. Out of respect for you concerning the days to come, I must wait, when all I want to do is make you mine.' He looked down earnestly at her, begging her to believe him, to trust his timing for their future.

'I spoke out of turn in the courthouse when I said I was going to go and get myself married. I didn't take it lightly. I meant every word, but I want this ghost laid to rest, and I am not honouring you as I should if I rush into this when I don't know where my next days will land me. My only thought is for you.'

Tears welled in her eyes. She reached up and touched his lips.

'I love you, Tobias. We can wait. I can wait. If you consider what is best for me, then I must also be thoughtful regarding you.'

And then she did what surprised him and made his heart soar. She laced her arms behind his neck, and pulled him down to kiss him.

He hoped that Parson Brown would be scarce a while longer yet.

Twenty-five

It was a day for soup making. Just when the cooler days seemed to have blown away, clouds came back to settle over the sea. A chill was in the rectory.

'We need to stoke that fire,' Mrs. Brown told Emma, rubbing her hands together. 'Then we'll set to with these vegetables and hang them in the pot over the fire. That mutton bone won't go to waste. We'll add it to the broth.'

'I'll start on cutting up what we need.'

'Let's have a pot of tea to warm us first. It's only early yet. We have all day to simmer the soup.'

So the two women sat and chatted. They skirted around what Emma most feared: that the killer had gone aground and that Tobias would once more face the noose. But at that moment Tobias was outside with Kevin rebuilding the picket fence that the kangaroos had knocked over. The animals had jumped over the palings to pick at the green vegetable tops. Mrs. Brown gestured through the door at the vegetable garden.

'I don't know why the animals bother, since they only seem intent on tramping on the root crops rather than eating them. The kangaroo possesses very unusual flavoured meat. I'd much rather mutton, pork or beef, and I only hope Kevin doesn't butcher the kangaroo he's promised. He said he'd share it with the parson and me.' Mrs. Brown grimaced. 'I told him he was welcome to the whole beast.'

'I haven't had the opportunity to try it.'

'It is like eating a mouthful of rat.' Mrs. Brown pulled a face.

'They're not a species related to the rat, surely?' Emma was dubious.

'Of course they are dear. You can tell from a mile away.'

'Some seem to enjoy it.'

The parson's wife shuddered. 'I just can't come at it. Like some horrifying rodent sitting up on its hind legs.' Mrs. Brown gave her best impression of the animal. Emma tried to stifle her laugh and failed.

'There's no kangaroo tail soup in this kitchen, Miss Colchester, I assure you,' the good woman promised on a jovial note, taking down the cauldron to fill.

Emma began peeling potatoes. The skins fell into the basin on the table in front of her as she concentrated on the task at hand, hardly noticing where her thoughts headed.

In her mind's eye she recollected the night she had stayed at the house on the banks of Hunter's River. Gideon had fought with the bushranger. Yet after Gideon had been shot, they had been unable to find him. Truth to tell, she didn't think that the overseer or any of the workers seemed too concerned for her fiancé's whereabouts, for how far could a drowned man travel downstream?

But she hadn't wanted his return, any more than the men had seemed to. She hadn't mourned when his body was brought from the depths of the river.

Gideon had visited her dreams at the Folly. They had buried him in a rough-hewn coffin, deep in the black soil on the banks of the river. But when he had appeared before her, it had seemed so real.

She had smelled the dank river, blood, and the wet worsted of his scarlet coat. He had stood beside the bed, watching her sleep. Leering grotesquely, his smile was opened to the gums, swollen and bleeding. Not quite the same as she had seen him in the raw coffin, perhaps, but far more frightening.

'You won't want me now. Will you, Emma dear?'

She had awoken to morning light coming from the high

sash windows. Of course, Gideon wasn't there. She knew he wouldn't be, couldn't be there. He was, after all dead and buried.

The body had been lowered into the cool pit. She had seen it with her own eyes. Yet after the burial, Emma remembered things she hadn't noticed about Gideon before. She recalled things about the man that hadn't been apparent at his graveside.

'I'm sorry for your loss, Miss Colchester, I really am, but I saw that body with my own eyes, and everyone else here did too, and I tell you now that the deceased was none other than Gideon Quinn. Why Miss, you know it was.' The overseer had looked worriedly at her.

But even after she had walked away from the overseer feeling foolish, she wondered why Gideon's hair had been more brown than grey, and why it curled around the ears just so. Perhaps the water was responsible for the curl. Perhaps the work of hungry fishes were responsible for the missing finger, because Emma had never noticed its lack before.

Emma set down the potato and began on another. She listened with half an ear as Mrs. Brown laughed at Emma's slow and meticulous peeling.

'Don't be too particular, Emma dear. None will be wasted. The fowls will have the skins boiled up and served with their pollard.'

'My mind is on other things,' Emma admitted.

'Of course it is. I understand. Say no more. You just take your time.'

But even as Emma turned to smile at the parson's wife, her mind was whisked away; to the court house this time, to the testimony of Jim; Jim who had witnessed murder at the Folly. He had seen the murderer that he said stalked Wallis Plains. An evil killer with a face half eaten in like the core of a rotten apple. Emma looked up. Mrs. Brown was speaking, but Emma didn't hear the words, because what she had feared before was now a tangible possibility. A very real prospect.

Gideon Quinn was not dead.

The potato dropped from Emma's fingers and rolled just past her feet. Dread swept over her. Nausea followed. Putting her hand out for support, she had to sit down before she fell.

The next moment Tobias was there beside her, his arms around her as she lay back against the settle. He pushed the hair from her brow and searched her face.

She smelled earth and honest toil. She saw the goodness in his face and the love he had for her. How could she have doubted his honesty even for a moment? Disappointment at herself was only momentary, before her mind flashed back to her fears.

'Emma, please tell me what's wrong.'

'It's Gideon,' she told him simply. 'Gideon's come back.'

Emma looked at Tobias and the parson, who had just walked in. She turned to Mrs. Brown then, wiping at tears that streamed down her face.

'What makes you say that?' Tobias's tone frightened her still more. Did he fear, too?

Mrs. Brown sat down beside her. 'Emma you have borne more in the last few months than many do in a lifetime. You, my dear, need a cup of tea and an ounce of rest.'

'I'll pray for peace,' the parson told her quietly. Emma glanced at the man. She wanted assurance, but his words held none.

'He came to me in a dream at the Folly, dripping like a wet dog. But it was real, Tobias. It was so real. Who else can it be but Gideon?'

'I'm going for the doctor,' he told her.

'Do you take what I say seriously?'

Tobias looked at her earnestly. 'I take it very seriously indeed.' Then he nodded to the parson and Mrs. Brown and left the cottage. Then there was the crunch of gravel beneath his feet on the gravel path before he closed the gate behind him.

'It's the truth,' she told the couple staring at her compassionately. 'Gideon is back. You know, he really never left at all.'

☫

Emma's behaviour was concerning. Tobias had never seen her act like that before. But it wasn't just her demeanour; it was what she had said.

'Gideon's come back.'

It made no sense, because Quinn was buried in the black sod at Wallis Plains. Yet Emma wasn't one for fancy. She wasn't given to histrionics. Emma had to be the steadiest soul he had ever met.

He couldn't believe that Quinn was lurking beneath the lintels of all and sundry at Wallis Plains. The murderer was someone else, surely? He recalled the glimpse of a soldier in a scarlet jacket as he had rowed Cecily downstream, but dismissed it.

Perhaps her uncle would work it out. He was a thoughtful person, just like his niece, and he was sure to figure out the reason for such an uncharacteristic outburst.

If anyone knew, whisperers might say she had lost her hold on reality. Mistress McGuiness would be such a one. Then he stopped in his tracks. Did he think she had let go of her sanity? No, no he didn't.

Tobias rapped at the surgeon's cottage. A convict with cropped hair answered the door.

'I'm Tobias Freeman. I've come to see the surgeon.'

'He's not at home,' a sharp voice called out before the girl could open her mouth to speak.

Tobias glanced through the half-opened door into the darkness of the cottage.

'He's not at home,' the maid repeated the words, making

ready to shut the door.

'He doesn't work Saturday afternoons.'

The serving girl looked sheepish. The voice from the interior called out again. 'You were told he's not at home!'

Tobias knew the shrill tones of Emma's aunt. Perhaps when the family had lost their daughter the mother had in some ways died as well. Still, that wasn't his problem; Emma was. Tobias pushed past the maid and walked into the cottage.

Emma's aunt was reclining on the settle. Even in the dimness, her contorted face told him she was livid.

'How dare you enter this house!' She bellowed at him, pulling herself up to a seated position. She stabbed an angry finger at the maid.

'You should never have let him in. Get out!' she told the girl.

The servant bobbed her mistress a curtsy before a hasty departure and seemed only too glad to do as she was bid.

'It wasn't her fault,' Tobias offered. 'I elbowed my way in.'

'She should have slammed the door in your face. And now that's just what I'm going to do.' The woman lurched after him.

'I just want to see the surgeon.' Tobias held his out his hands in appeasement. It made no difference. The woman advanced.

But at the sound of the cottage door, they both looked up. It was the doctor. The woman's hands dropped to her sides.

'Ah, Tobias, Matilda said you were here. I was around the back doing a spot of gardening.' His hands attested to the truth of his words. 'It's a calming pastime, don't you know?' His steady smile held up, as though nothing was amiss, but he was altogether too jovial.

'It is good to see you,' Tobias told him earnestly, 'but I came here for Emma's sake.'

'Emma's ill?'

Tobias sought to reassure him. 'It's more of a precaution.'

'I gathered it was an emergency, the way you pushed your way in here,' Emma's aunt rounded on him.

'And I'm glad you did,' Emma's uncle told him. 'You've done the right thing. Wait a moment while I clean my hands and then we'll go.'

Tobias didn't want to be left in the cottage with Emma's aunt spitting her poison and took the man's lead.

'I'll wait for you at the parsonage and let Emma know you're on your way. Good day to you madam, I'm sorry to have disturbed your afternoon.' But Tobias received no acknowledgement from Emma's aunt.

The last thing he saw before she closed the door behind him was a baleful stare, no flicker of benevolence that he could see.

Twenty-six

'Now tell me, Emma, explain if you can, what ails you.'

Emma looked into her uncle's eyes. So much hurt he had suffered, and suffered still. He appeared more hollow eyed than he had before the trial, if that was possible, yet here he was continuing to serve others without complaint.

'I'm afraid.'

'Worry can make anyone unwell,' he conceded. 'You are bound to be worried, considering Tobias's trial. With still no culprit to be found, everyone in the community is concerned.'

'And well they should be,' she whispered, 'but what frightens me, Uncle George, is that the murderer is Gideon Quinn.'

Her uncle thought about this. He ruminated on the idea. A frown rested a heavy hand upon his brow.

'Gideon Quinn was buried before either of the murders, Emma,' he reminded her gently. Emma put her head in her hands.

'I know there was a burial,' she said. 'I saw the man they said was Gideon, eaten by the fishes and put to rest in a coffin by the bank, but afterwards, I wondered. I told my concerns to the overseer, but understandably he dismissed them. The man could have been Gideon. Yet there were things I noticed about him that were not quite right.'

Her uncle was looking at her with concern. 'But what makes you think that officer Quinn is the perpetrator of such unspeakable acts?'

'I dreamed of him. He spoke to me. I woke up but he was gone. I thought at the time that it was just the workings of an overwrought mind. Now I believe he really had been standing by the bed as I slept.' She shivered. 'I believe that he is alive still, and that he is the culprit the witness attested to committing the crime at the Folly.'

Perhaps he was Euphemie's murderer too.

'Why do you think that he would do such a thing?'

'Gideon Quinn was a liar and a thief.'

'That doesn't make him a murderer,' he reminded her.

Emma spun on her seat to face him more fully. She had begun to shake. 'That's not the end of it though, I was told that he bludgeoned a convict to death.'

Uncle George's eyes narrowed.

'He made Tobias dig the grave and throw the body in the hole he fashioned. He told him that if he didn't do as he was bid, that he would point the blame in Tobias's direction.'

Her uncle blinked, pushing the glasses flat against the bridge of his nose. Emma continued. 'You see, there's not one body down by the Hunter River. There's two.'

'I can't believe that he would have done any woman to death,' Her uncle was unable to finish his sentence. He cleared his throat. 'Why, he ate supper at our table many times. He knew Euphemie as an acquaintance. Furthermore, what man would attack his mother? I'm sorry Emma, but I think your fears are askew.'

'And the death of the convict?'

'Knocking an unruly felon over the head is vastly different from attacking a guiltless woman. But regardless of what I think, I will walk you to the barracks and wait for you there,' her uncle told her seriously. 'You need to speak to the commandant. And if what you have imparted to me is of any help in finding the criminal of such heinous crimes,' he faltered and steadied his emotions. 'If any information you give brings my daughter and Cecily Quinn justice, then your efforts will not be in vain. But I do not share your idea that Gideon is alive and well and is the instigator of such mayhem. I just can't.'

Emma squeezed her uncle's hand. 'I'm sorry to dredge the

hurt up.' Emma told him.

Uncle George smiled. Resigned to sorrow. 'It never goes away, my dear. You can hardly make it worse.'

Emma and her Uncle George went to search for Tobias. He was in the church with Parson Brown. A few of the pews in the convicts' gallery had weakened, and Tobias was plying his hand to restoring them. He looked up, and seeing Emma and her uncle, put down his tools and straightened, descending the stairs.

'I am going to see the commandant. Uncle George will go with me as a support, and wait until I have had office with him.'

'Why?' Tobias wanted to know. Emma recounted her fears.

'I won't mention anything to put you at risk, Tobias.' Emma took his hand and held it.

'I am, and have already been at risk,' he reminded her. 'I still am. And if you're talking about Allan Campbell, buried secretly under the sod, then tell him that too.'

'No,' Emma fretted. 'I won't mention that.'

'I bore witness to that crime. Now I'll bear witness to the truth.'

'But you cannot prove that it wasn't you,' Emma cried, and she heard the fear in her own voice. Parson Brown's face showed concern.

'If God is with us, who can stand against us?'

'I won't see Tobias martyred for someone else's crime.' The parson and Uncle George exchanged worried glances.

'It must be done, Emma. I cannot have the guilt of that man's death forever in my heart, because I was too afraid to speak up for what was right. Don't think I don't know what's at stake, Emma. Don't think I'm not afraid. But I won't live in fear of tomorrow when there's a criminal to find today. And if Quinn is alive – just if – then as God is my judge, I won't stand by and allow him the benefit of life when he has been the instrument of death.'

How could she argue with that? Emma walked with Tobias and her uncle towards the barracks. She was weighed down by dread, yet Tobias fairly strode out, his purpose clear, his mind driven. Emma could do little but hurry along at his side.

The tang of horseflesh, manure, hempen rope and leather met her nostrils as they walked into the barracks. There were the sounds of distant commands, of boots upon gravel, and Emma felt ill. She did not want to be here. She did not want to implicate Tobias in any way.

'Miss Colchester,' Officer Gray said. 'It's always a pleasant surprise to see you.' Emma was brought back to the moment. Tobias made an unpleasant sound, though neither of the gentlemen addressed one another.

'I've come to talk with the commandant,' Emma explained.

'He's taking tea at the moment. Perhaps you could talk with me?'

'I'll wait outside with your uncle,' Tobias told her quietly. And then more loudly, 'The air has grown stale in here. Bad smells always make me feel queasy.'

Emma flushed. It was blatantly obvious that Tobias's rudeness was directed solely at the officer. She watched Tobias walk out the door. Turning back to Octavius Gray, she noted his cold disregard of Tobias's back.

'That man may well have been given his freedom, but I've always thought: once a convict, always a convict. Mingle in polite society, they cannot. Stand out like ... anyway, as I was saying, I'd be more than happy to assist you.'

'Mr. Freeman is a perfect gentleman, I assure you,' Emma was quick to say.

'Although we may needs agree to disagree on that point, Miss Colchester, you on the other hand are obviously a perfect lady.'

Emma looked away at the audacity of the man's compliment.

She cleared her throat as though it was her who had spoken the forthright words.

'I'd be obliged if you'd allow me to wait here until he's finished taking his tea.'

'Why of course you may wait here, Miss Colchester. Is there any refreshment that I can offer you?'

'Thank you Officer Gray, but no.'

Emma prepared to sit when the commandant walked through the door with a ready smile.

'Well, well, Miss Colchester. If I had known you were coming, I would have waited to take tea with you. To what do I owe the pleasure of this visit?'

His presence eased her fears a little, and Emma smiled in reply. 'Commandant Morisset, I'm afraid there is nothing pleasant in my being here. I've come on an urgent private matter. Although now I cannot help but wonder if I am on a fool's errand. I wonder if we might ... '

'Please, step inside my office.' And then to Officer Gray with a jocular tone, 'I have all the time in the world for this young lady. I hope you have extended her every courtesy whilst she was good enough to wait for my audience?'

'I've only been here a short time,' Emma assured the commandant. 'Officer Gray was happy to be of assistance.'

'Then we can conclude that the man is no fool, and may make commandant himself, one day. Still, I try not to compliment you too many times a day on that sharp mind of yours. Isn't that right, Officer Gray?'

'Yes, sir. That's right.'

The commandant followed Emma into his office then closed the door, at once serious. He dispensed with his wit as he unbuttoned the neck of his coat, and offered her a chair with concern.

Dispensing with preamble, she told him why she was there.

'As I recount these fears, Commandant Morisset, I realise how ludicrous this all sounds.'

The commandant dragged a hand over his jaw. For a moment he made no comment. But then he asked, 'Why would Gideon Quinn kill his own mother?'

'My uncle wondered the same thing, and it's a pertinent question I hadn't thought to ask myself. However, I do remember her saying she had not seen her son for many years.'

'Yet surely if he had stumbled upon her in his own house, he would have realised who the woman was? Miss Colchester, I think very highly of you, I hope you know that,' the commandant began. 'I hold you in the utmost respect. But I feel that it's likely that the waterlogged body that was fished out of the river was Gideon Quinn. Whomever is stalking Wallis Plains cannot be him. Even if he were alive, I don't see him murdering anyone for the mere thrill.'

'He was in possession of contraband. It's in the main chamber at the house he had built at Wallis Plains. I'm sorry I've only just thought to make you aware of the fact. I stumbled upon it when I was there.'

'Ah, so that's where it went.' The commandant nodded. 'Still, that does not make him guilty of slaying innocent women.'

Regardless of his wishes, Emma couldn't find it in herself to embroil Tobias, however much more credence it gave to the story she told. All she could do was state her fears.

'I came here to voice my concerns, which sound silly now I admit, and yet I have the unshakable feeling that Gideon lives.'

'Please don't feel foolish, Miss Colchester. Yet understand that unless I find further evidence to support your suspicions, I'm afraid my hands are tied. I'm sorry if I sound like a cad. It's not my intention.'

Emma sat wordlessly in front of the commandant. The voice

of Allan Campbell prompted her conscience, yet she remained silent. Although she trusted the commandant, she knew that he would be obliged to make an inquiry into the death of the young Scottish convict. Tobias was the only one who knew of his death, and no one could verify the truth of his words.

Twenty-seven

The commandant stared out the window of his office towards the harbour. A day bright with sun, gulls careened over brilliant waves. He had breakfasted alone, as was his wont. He turned to put down the tea bowl in its saucer. He fumbled and the cup clattered. The noise of it rattled his nerves. He went back over Miss Colchester's extraordinary story.

The young woman was far from being looked upon as a fanciful creature by anyone in the colony, and yet the frightening tale she had told him was fantastic. She had been engaged to marry Gideon Quinn, yet it would appear she hadn't thought any more of him than anyone in the constabulary had. But being unpopular didn't make the man a murderer.

He would be the last one to believe that she would try and pin such a heinous crime on Quinn, merely because of lacklustre affection. Not even for the sake of letting Tobias Freeman off the hook. So if that was the case, why did she think Quinn was the murderer? Was it just irrational fear she was a victim of? Or was there something else she knew that made her make such an impossible accusation? He bit on his thumbnail. It was ragged. He made it more so. He took it down to the quick and then went on to his pointer finger. Something had to be done to find out the truth regarding the murderer in their midst.

A knock at the door, and Officer Gray put his head around it. 'Finished breakfast, Commandant Morisset?' Gray asked.

The commandant waved vaguely at the half-eaten remains sitting on the breakfast tray.

'Don't worry about the tray yet Gray. Sit down. I need to talk to someone.' The commandant joined him, and dived in without preamble.

'What are your thoughts on Miss Emma Colchester?'

'She's a beauty,' Gray shrugged.

Gray's offhand praise belied his true interest, but the flush of the young man's cheeks told the commandant what he had already deduced.

The commandant waved it away. That wasn't what he was asking.

'Let me explain,' and the commandant began the story he had just heard.

'Have you considered that Miss Colchester might well be overwrought? Suffering a breakdown, as it were?'

'Look at it this way. Miss Colchester champions that big-mouthed ex convict as though he is all sunshine and light. She doesn't want to see him hanged for those murders. I'm not saying she is trying to protect him by means fair or foul, but it looks as though she's under duress. Maybe she knows he's guilty and it's pushing her over the edge.'

The commandant considered the young man before him and sighed.

'I'm not sure where this inquiry is headed, I really don't.' Another knock at the door and the commandant was informed that there was a lady there to see him. Officer Gray smirked.

'Must be your lucky week, sir.' The commandant gave him a droll look, and waited for the visitor to be ushered in as Gray left his office.

The woman wasn't elderly, not yet was she young. He couldn't precisely gauge what her age was, so weathered was her face. Her work-worn hands were worse. One thing he did pick up on in an instant was that she was angry.

'I came here a month ago and since then I have heard nothing, nothing at all from the constabulary.'

'Concerning what, may I ask, madam?' She looked at him as

though he was a dunderhead.

'My husband has been missing for months, and I've seen neither hide nor hair of him. Now what do you think about that?'

'That's very unfortunate, madam, and you have my apologies.'

The woman harrumphed. 'Unfortunate? Oh, you think so?' The commandant grimaced inwardly.

'Perhaps, madam, he sought greener pastures? I apologise for my plain speaking, but he would not be the first.'

'Not my John, he was the best of any husband that ever a woman could want.' And then the woman began crying. The commandant hung his head a little.

'What line of work was your husband in?'

'He was a lieutenant in His Majesty's service!'

He had been told nothing of the affair. None of the soldiers had reported anyone missing, from either Newcastle nor Wallis Plains. But someone needed to own up to the blunder. The commandant flushed.

'Please accept my apologies, madam. I was not informed that you had been here concerning your husband. I don't know why the constabulary at Wallis Plains hasn't thought to bring the matter to our attention either. What is your husband's name?'

'Lieutenant John Thackeray.' Commandant Morisset handed her his handkerchief, poured her a tumbler of water from the jug at his elbow, and waited for her to compose herself.

He tried to recall the name of anyone in the constabulary who had put in for a transfer, but recollection of a soldier by the name of Thackeray eluded him. The ledger, however, told him that it was indeed the truth.

'I wonder, madam, if you would be able to tell me what your husband looked like? What was his hair-colour, his build? Had he any distinguishing marks?'

And the commandant listened as she told him everything about the man she loved, from the way he laughed to the way he liked his mutton cooked. When she had finished, he looked up.

'What did the constabulary at Wallis Plains tell you?'

'Gave me some story about being undermanned and underpaid. Said that he had obviously got his start here in Newcastle and had left early with a mind to get things sorted. But we weren't meant to come until after winter, and what man goes fishing and forgets to tell his missus that he's going to set up house? He never came back for me, commandant.'

The commandant shook his head. 'Rest assured madam, that a search will be carried out, just as soon as I can make the order. I give you my word that your husband's disappearance will not be taken lightly. I hope you can rest on that assertion.'

'Thank you, Commandant Morisset. If I could have spoken to you in the first place, then I wouldn't have had to come all this way a second time. It's not easy to make the journey here, and I have waited with no news. That carrot-headed nowt I spoke to hardly knew the time of day.'

The commandant cringed a little. 'Do you recall his name?'

'No, but he was Irish. I remember that.'

Rory Ferguson? The young man's wife was expecting a child. Was that why he had been air-headed of late? Between that and the tragedy at their doorstep, it was more than likely that the lad had forgotten to write up the woman's concerns. Still, it was not good enough. Now he would have to find answers for this woman. He'd also be having a stern heart-to-heart with Rory Ferguson.

'Your husband's disappearance will not be filed and forgotten, not this time.' Then he escorted the woman from his office. 'Gray, find Rory Ferguson and tell him I want to see him.'

'He's not here, sir.'

'What do you mean, he's not here?' The commandant was

finding himself increasingly put out.

'His missus had a fall, and being in a delicate condition, he came to ask leave to stay home for the day.'

Family matters or not, the boy needed to smarten up. He needed to iron this out, and it couldn't wait another minute. 'You need to go and get him.'

'Now, Commandant Morisset?'

'I want it done now, without delay. Regardless of his wife's condition, I need to know if it was he who neglected to document the disappearance of John Thackeray.'

When Octavius Gray returned with Rory Ferguson, the lad had already been informed of the commandant's gripe, and was flushing to the roots of his scalp.

'Tell me, why did you neglect to make record of the absence of a Lieutenant John Thackeray?' The russet-nut thought for a moment, glowed a deeper shade of red and remained silent.

'I asked you a question.'

'I'm afraid it's a little hazy in my memory, sir.'

'A woman came here from Wallis Plains with the news that the man of the house had disappeared, and you tell me that you don't have the foggiest notion? What excuse can you give me to justify your neglect, Lieutenant Ferguson?'

'I can give you none, Commandant Morisset.'

'Can you recall someone by the name of Thackeray who was looking to start here in the spring?'

'No Commandant Morisset, I'm afraid I can't.'

'I can't help but wonder who is expecting, Ferguson, your wife or you. Since you've had news of this child, you seem to have lost your wits. Perhaps a temporary cut in your salary might help you to be more careful in future.' He dismissed the lieutenant and stewed some more.

His mind turned back to Mrs. Thackeray's fears for her

husband. The man had been missing for months. That a soldier of the crown could have been conveniently forgotten because of someone's neglect of duty was appalling. Why had the constabulary been so lax? It angered him. The man had amounted to more than just the scribbling of the constabulary's daily entries; he was someone's husband.

He understood rules, he understood discipline, and though he had been given no information regarding Thackeray's absence, he felt that in some way he was responsible. It rankled that the buck stopped with him. Such a miscarriage of duty ought never to have happened. He would solve the mystery surrounding Thackeray, and give the woman the answers that she needed. The answers she deserved.

Then as he sat and thought, chewing on one of the remaining fingernails long enough to be bitten off, he recalled what Miss Colchester had told him about her concerns for the body which had been interred.

'I have the unshakable feeling that Gideon is alive.'

One soldier was missing. He'd been missing for as long as Quinn had been buried. Yet if Quinn wasn't the one buried on the banks of the Hunter River, was Lieutenant Thackeray's body the one six feet down in the black soil?

Twenty-eight

Jim stood with Tam outside the Wheatsheaf Arms. Tankards in hand, they looked out upon the Hunter River. In late winter afternoons such as this, mist rose from the water. A ghostly body that twisted through the trees, pointing the way downstream.

Jim's thoughts drifted with the fog as it blanketed the landscape. There was a silence, a stillness that was almost oppressive. Jim fancied as though the moist air would fill his lungs to overwhelm him.

He glanced in the direction of the big house. He couldn't see it. There were trees and some few miles that separated it from his sight, but he imagined he could feel it.

It was brooding. It was strangely menacing. The darkness that he had witnessed probably tainted its very walls. He would not work there, no matter how much money he was offered.

'You still keen to join in the search party, Tam?' His voice sounded far away.

'Aye, I am. They're putting on a free lunch.' Tam was animated.

'You're an old skinflint Tam. Anyway, everyone knows there's no such thing.'

'Publican just told me everyone's assembling here at the crack of dawn. Then at noon he's going to put on a spread; mutton and damper.'

'Still need to buy your own grog, you know. The innkeeper just wants to make more income.'

'Suppose so,' Tam shrugged. 'Still, there's nothing wrong with that. It's called good business. Anyway, I'm not going to snig out timber tomorrow. I'd rather chew the fat and look for the phantom that killed the old girl.'

'How many times do I have to tell you? It was no phantom. The murderer was real enough. A ghost can't strangle the life out of a body, you know. Besides, do you think every redcoat from here to the Coal River would search for an apparition? I don't think so. All the king's men will arrive here tomorrow morning, and it's not just to break bread with the publican.' Jim quaffed his ale. 'I need another beer.'

As he turned to walk inside the pub he heard Tam say, 'I was only having a lark.'

He was tired of people looking at him like he was having himself on.

When he emerged from the public house once more, he was a little more relaxed. Ale in hand, he stepped onto the porch to find that Tam had gone home. He hadn't even bothered to say goodbye. It wasn't Jim's fault if he didn't like being made a laughing stock. He'd simply had enough. They would sit up when the commandant captured the murderer.

He doubted that anyone in the colony realised just how much danger they were in. *He* did, and he wasn't afraid to admit to anyone that dreams plagued his sleep most nights, and that he found himself looking over his shoulder even when the sun was high.

Yet much more like a hero now, he determined that it would be him that would catch the cold-blooded fiend, he who would bring justice to Wallis Plains.

Hops made a man look at a situation in a more fearless light. It fortified a man. Aye, beer was a stout friend. He belched and stared into the receding day with satisfaction.

The mist had crept a little closer. Jim felt the dampness on his cheeks. Relaxed now though, he breathed in the chill, thinking of the morrow. He imagined seeing the admiration on the face of Commandant Morisset as he regaled the men with Jim's prowess.

Jim formulated a plan as he downed one more beer, then began the long walk to the big house.

The building loomed threatening. The eyes of the windows bore down on him, but half a dozen tankards of ale had given him courage to carry on. Still, he made his way cautiously enough around the outbuildings.

He smelled the fragrant scent of lit kindling. Burning twigs gave off a sharp tang. Jim frowned a little and looked up. There was smoke rising from the chimney. He peered hard up towards the roof. He couldn't only smell the smoke, he could see it, and he wondered who was staying at the house.

Light had faded. Darkness was a stealthy cloak and he let it wrap itself around him. He wanted to know who was in the house, and the only way to do it was go up and look. A shiver licked up his back and he came out in goose-flesh. Jim hunkered deeper into the shadow.

He tiptoed into one of the outbuildings and found an axe resting against the wall. He clutched it to his side, prepared to use it as a weapon. He scanned the windows of the home. His heart was jumping in his chest as Jim made his way to the porch.

There was indeed a fire roaring in the grate, and beside it a young black girl crouched. She wore nothing but a kangaroo pelt around her shoulders, and just as extraordinary, held a lady's parasol above her head. Jim blushed to look at the young woman, although she was hardly more than a girl, and he saw that her stomach was swollen by pregnancy. Saw too, that she was in some distress.

It was a strange spectacle, and even as he watched he saw her stand up and clutch at her stomach. Her hands went to her groin and came away red and slick with blood. Jim blushed and turned away.

He heard her call out. There was someone within the house,

She directed her gaze above stairs and Jim's own followed. But just as she fell to the floor, the person he had wanted and yet dreaded to see, made his leisurely way down the stairs. The murderer was making free in the house.

The man looked down at the girl dispassionately. He lifted a pewter rum cup to quaff a measure as she whimpered upon the ground. Even as Jim watched the widening pool of blood at her feet, he knew that whatever was happening to the expectant young mother was far from normal. He didn't know what was worse: the vision of the girl haemorrhaging upon the floor, or the careless bystander watching her bleed to death. Jim was powerless to help.

Then the fiend tipped her head and helped her to drink. Another mouthful and another, and the rum trickled down her chin. As Jim looked on the poor girl groaned. She looked towards where Jim stood, as if she saw him watching from his vantage point, before her eyes rolled back and she collapsed upon the floor.

Jim felt sick. As if his lifeblood was draining away. And still he stood helpless as a child. He hardly realised that he had dropped the axe, until it hit his foot to fall sideways onto the porch. The killer looked up, and as Jim stared in horrified wonder, the villain turned his face to meet Jim's eye.

There was no humanity in that gaze, no warmth in the pallid stare, and Jim looked back for what seemed an eternity before he thought to move.

Sobriety had returned. Courage fled. Jim turned and careened away from the porch and into the night. As he ran he wondered if the sound of thundering footfalls were his own desperate feet, or whether it was the hammering of his heart.

He ran until the breath burned from his throat down to his lungs. He stumbled forward with no thought save the will to live. When he reached his own cottage, he fell into the place, gasping as he bolted the door. Then he turned to get the bread knife that rested on the hearthstone, and sat with his back to the wall until almost daybreak. It wasn't until the birds lifted chorus that he felt himself lulled.

He slept until a knock sounded on the door.

'Open the door, Jim,' Tam called out. 'The search is about to begin.'

Jim sat bolt upright, eyes opening on a start. He stumbled to the door and unbolted it in relief. 'What's up, Jimmy my man? You look like you've seen a ghost. You've had the devil of a night, by the looks of you.'

Jim let out a sigh of relief. He slumped down on the stump he used as a chair. 'Tam, I've never been so glad to see anyone in all my born days.'

Tam looked at him, then at the cold fireplace.

'Och, you aren't even ready. You've slept in.'

Jim looked at his friend. 'Tam, I don't even know if I've slept.' He grabbed a crust of stale damper and bit down half-heartedly as he closed the cottage door behind him. 'This is hardly worth the effort it takes to chew it,' he mumbled, throwing it wide. A magpie from a nearby tree swooped down in an instant and took the discarded bread in its beak before it flew back to its place in the trees.

Tam looked at him askance.

'I can't eat. It sticks in my gullet.'

'You must have a hangover, man,' Tam chuckled and clapped Jim on the back. Jim looked around. The bush was quiet. Just the sigh of a cool breeze that riffled his shirt tails. He wasn't going to tell Tam what had befallen him. At that moment he didn't have the words to explain the sad recollection of the young dark girl on the floor of the big house, dismay on her face at the blood between her naked legs.

No woman, black or white, deserved the careless disregard that the redcoat had served her with. It had been the killer – on that, Jim would stake his life.

Why he hadn't murdered the girl, Jim had no idea. But then again, he hadn't exactly tried to save her life either.

Let the commandant rout out the felon. Jim had little courage now. A belly of beer under the belt had only given him grandiose ideas. But it was through him alone that the search would be finished a lot sooner than the men waiting to begin the day were bargaining for. Jim walked up to the first officer he saw.

'What do you want?' The officer gave him the once over.

'I need to see the commandant,' Jim said.

'He's busy.' The soldier hardly bothered to glance at Jim as he spoke.

Jim hadn't slept, he had eaten nothing but a mouthful of crust, and if this officer had been at the court hearing, he would know just who Jim was.

'I'm the one who witnessed the murder,' Jim condescended to say.

The officer looked down his nose, speculating. 'I for one would never trust the witness of a drunk.'

'I'm not a drunk,' Jim protested, his cheeks burning indignation.

'You smell like the bottom of a piss-pot,' the officer sniffed.

Jim's jaw fell slack. 'I had a few drinks last night, I'll admit that, but that Irishman never murdered the old girl in the big house, and I won't say anything different.'

'Well, I just hope we find the culprit, otherwise your oath will look as hollow as those sunken cheeks of yours.'

Jim touched his face without thought. It wasn't always easy to put a meal on the table when he was only cooking for one.

He supposed he looked like he could do with a good feed, but then, it was nothing to do with this soldier who couldn't treat a man with common courtesy. Jim straightened his spine and squared his shoulders.

'When will the commandant be free to talk to me?' Jim began a second time.

'Now look, unless you have something of real importance to tell the commandant, you will be wasting his time as well as your own. Commandant Morisset is a very busy man, and if I'm any judge of character, you don't appear to have worked an honest day in your life.'

Jim pulled off his hat and threw it at the officer's feet.

'Now listen here, I work for my bread. I've neither done nor said aught that gives you the right to speak to me as though I were nothing more than the dirt beneath your feet. I witnessed foul murder in that house yonder, and I swore on the Good Book that what I said was the whole truth and nothing but the truth. But while I'm at it, perhaps I'll hand you another bit of honesty, and it's this ... '

'Is there a problem, gentlemen?' Both men turned around. It was the senior officer that Jim remembered from the court hearing. Commandant Morisset, the man he wanted to see.

'This gentleman wanted to see you, Commandant Morisset, but I thought that you might be still breaking your fast.'

Jim looked at the unhelpful officer as he spoke, and recollected that he had met this man before. Jim squinted in slow-dawning remembrance.

'I remember you,' Jim rounded, one finger punctuating each word.

'I didn't realise I was so memorable,' the officer quipped. The commandant held up a hand for silence. Jim ignored the gesture and continued his tirade.

'On the day of the trial I went to the barracks to see the commandant, and you told me the same thing you did just now. You told me that the commandant was busy, even though I explained to you that I had information regarding a murder at Wallis Plains. You knew Commandant Morisset was in court listening to the trial of the Irishman, and if it wasn't for the fact that I had nothing better to do than sit down and listen to the trial, an innocent man would surely have been hanged!'

'Innocent man be damned. The man is a convicted criminal made lucky. You speak as though he is a son of the gentry, when Tobias Freeman is nothing more than a petty criminal at best, and a cold-blooded ... ' The redcoat stopped speaking as the ex-convict in question stepped in front of him.

'Do you have business with me?'

'No I do not.'

'Only, I heard my name bandied about and I thought that if you weren't gossiping like an old woman that you might perhaps have wanted to pass the time of day. As it is, I'm here to help catch a villain, and I don't have a gentleman's leisure to stop and chat.

'Top of the morning to you, sir.' Freeman doffed his hat to the commandant and Jim. He shook Jim's hand solemnly before he walked away.

The commandant nodded in reply to Freeman, and turned to Jim.

'I believe I like that Irishman,' Jim said.

Commandant Morisset tried to stifle a smile. He failed.

'He does seem to have that effect on the majority of people.'

'Not all,' the officer said, wanting to make a nuisance of himself again it would seem. Jim looked at the snivelling, trumped-up, circus ape he later learned was named Octavius Gray.

'You wanted to talk with me, my good man?' the commandant

asked. Jim nodded and ignored the officer in the red coat.

'Last night I went to the big house ... '

'The Folly?' the officer wanted to know. 'What business did you have in going there?' Jim pretended not to hear him.

'Continue,' the commandant said.

Jim hesitated. 'I wanted to catch the man responsible for the death I witnessed.' The commandant's brows rose.

'A risky business, I should think.'

'Foolhardy,' Octavius Gray agreed.

Jim glared at him and then went on. 'I've seen him more than once. I've seen him once from afar, and then out in the paddock over yonder at dusk.'

'It could equally have been someone else.'

Jim looked at Octavius Gray pointedly. 'It could have been, but it wasn't. So I went to the big house to see if he had gone back there.'

'Why should he go there?'

Jim took a deep breath and tried counting to three. Jim spoke slowly. The imbecile was either hard of hearing, or short on brains.

'I don't know why he would go there. We aren't on speaking terms. He sees me. I run. That's how it tends to pan out in the heat of the moment. But this time, I thought that if I found him, I'd rout him out, and have him trussed up by the time you got here. But then I saw him, and I ran.' Jim shrugged sheepishly.

The monkey showed his teeth. Jim took it for a smile; a smart arse one at that.

'Officer Gray, that's enough,' the commandant warned, his opinion of the man seemed to sour with each interaction. The commandant wasn't smirking at Jim's questionable courage, and Jim was thankful for that. His cheeks burned regardless.

So Jim told the commandant what he had seen. He left

nothing out, and when the commandant heard the last of Jim's encounter, he called all the men close.

'It appears that the murderer was seen in the house yesterday evening. If we advance quickly and quietly, I believe we will have the culprit faster than we had previously hoped. I want silence from every man, and I'm asking for stealth. When we have our quarry, we'll share a fine repast with the innkeeper.' The mob made comments of appreciation.

'Remember that the person whom we seek has no respect for life, and that includes your own, so be on your guard.'

They made the slow march along the river. They approached as one, in battle formation. With pistols, bayonets and broomsticks; pitchfork, pick and hoe. When they neared the property, the only sound was the breeze sighing through the needles of she-oaks above their heads. Jim shuddered involuntarily.

'Someone just walked over your grave,' Tam said.

'I hope not.'

The commandant, ahead of them, turned his gaze in a slow arc. He took in the glance of every man. Then training his eyes in the direction of their quarry, motioned them to proceed.

'In the name of King George!' the commandant called at the foot of the porch steps. 'Come out and give yourself up!'

But there was silence in the house. There was nothing and no one to be found of any interest in the grand house save a few kegs of rum, lettered: God Save the King.

'But he was in this very parlour,' Jim protested, looking desperately around. 'There was blood pooling all round the girl.'

'There's no trace of any blood that I can see,' someone ventured.

'Floor seems damp,' another one said.

'It's been raining. Roof might have leaked,' was the reply.

'It appears that the fox has flown the coop, and left us once more to cluck like nervous hens.' The commandant spoke to no one in particular, but a few men glanced over their shoulders at him. Most just stared at Jim.

Jim walked out into the brightness of the day.

'The Folly has made a fool of you,' the ape turned to grin as he passed him, and at that moment it was Jim who felt like he had been made a monkey of.

Twenty-nine

'Be on your guard, men,' the commandant warned. 'The suspect could still be lurking where we least expect.'

'You believe the word of a drunk, sir?' Gray asked. The commandant glanced at him.

'As a matter of fact, Gray, I do. If the man has a drinking problem, it doesn't automatically signify he has a problem with the truth.'

'I realise that, Commandant Morisset, but fear and the darkness does strange things to a man; that and a fraction too much ale. He could well be mistaking the criminal for someone else entirely. I don't understand why that Irishman Freeman is on the loose, as he supposedly helps us look for the murderer. He should be under lock and key until such time as the suspect is found. *If* a suspect is found.'

'Commandant Morisset!' The commandant turned at the sound of a raised voice.

'We've found a body!' Rory Ferguson called.

The body of a young woman, covered by a cursory screen of shrubs, was curled up like a cold child. Although not much effort had been put into the task, it was a burial of sorts.

'That's her!' Jim cried. 'That's the young girl I saw in the house.' The commandant sighed and straightened, glad that this part of Jim's story added up.

'She needs a proper burial,' someone said.

The commandant considered. 'She ought to be taken to her people. Have a stretcher made and take her downstream. The tribe can't be more than an hour away by boat. They won't have travelled far from where they were yesterday.'

'What if they try to spear us, sir?' one of the young soldiers remonstrated.

'They'll know that you come in peace when they see who you are returning to their care. But have your wits about you, and keep your gun close by your side.'

'Jackie knows their lingo, Commandant Morisset. He's right here, with the party. Shall I fetch him?'

'Yes. Make sure to take him with you to explain.'

The commandant turned away from the lifeless body. Why had the girl been in the Folly? There was a parasol opened above her head as if to shade her from the sun or her nakedness. A few men began to cut saplings for a stretcher, but the rest of the party made to follow the commandant back to the inn.

'Make sure to fortify yourselves before you head off. You need lunch as much as the rest of us.'

The commandant wasn't sure if Jackie understood, but he nodded nonetheless, teeth flashing white against the darkness of his skin.

'Gwandalan, mije tarti. Bomburra.' Jackie smiled down at the dead girl as though to reassure her. 'Awabakal,' Jackie looked at the commandant as if to explain, thumping his chest. 'Worimi,' he gestured to the girl.

The commandant didn't understand. There was so much he couldn't fathom right now. He walked towards the public house, considering the widow who had come to see him. She deserved to know the whereabouts of her husband.

At a commotion behind him, he stopped to turn around. He saw to his disgust but not surprise that Octavius Gray and Tobias Freeman were locked in combat. It looked as though the Irishman had the upper hand. The commandant withdrew his pistol and shot a warning into the air. Neither of the two men heeded. The commandant advanced.

'Pull them apart!' he ordered. 'What is going on here? We cannot find a killer, but that we have to try and slaughter one another?'

'He tried to cut my throat!' Gray cried. 'The filthy Irishman made to stick me. I knew he was nothing but a cur hell-bent on murder.'

Tobias Freeman hollered at the insult, wrenching away from the two men who held him. He went for Gray again, but the commandant stood in his path.

'Don't do it.'

'He's a liar,' Tobias growled. 'He wanted me to hang for crimes I never committed. And now that his wishes are going awry, he's trying to pin this on me.'

'Oh, for the love of God ... ' Gray tried to goad Tobias.

'You're a blasphemous liar, and you know nothing of the love of God.' He turned to the commandant with a plea. 'He made a disparaging remark about Emma – Miss Colchester that is – said that when he's hanged me by the neck, he'll make sure he looks after her real well. I understood his meaning. I went for him, aye, as any man would. I pulled a knife from his grasp and dropped it to the ground, but it was he who yanked it out of hiding, not me, and well he knows it.'

'Did anyone hear the altercation?' the commandant sighed, dragging a hand through his hair. A curl fell back down over his forehead, and he swept it from his eyes in frustration. 'Does anyone know what went on?' Rory Ferguson stepped forward.

'I saw Tobias with the knife in his hand, but then I saw him throw it to the ground before he struck out at officer Gray.'

'You see!' Octavius Gray yelled. 'There's a witness to prove the knife was in his hand!'

'Aye and why wouldn't I have used it if I had a mind to stick you?' Tobias demanded.

The commandant looked first at Gray and then at Tobias. 'I'm afraid you will need to head back to Newcastle, Mr. Freeman.

Doubtless you're wanted at home.'

Tobias threw a look at Gray, then nodded.

'And you,' the commandant whispered to Octavius Gray, 'if you so much as cause another stir, I will see you court-marshaled.'

'How can you take his word against mine? An officer of the crown?'

The commandant saw an emotion akin to hate shine out of the man's eyes before he thought to veil it.

'I have not taken sides,' the commandant reasoned, 'I have merely separated you from one another. One might say that behaviour like that from an Irish ex convict isn't anything untoward, but from one of the king's men, it is inexcusable, and I won't have it.'

As the commandant turned to walk away, Rory Ferguson caught up and handed him the knife. 'I thought it would be safer in your hands, sir,' the lieutenant said.

The commandant looked down at the weapon. It was well made. Fine steel and smooth wood. Although there was no initial engraved on its surface, it was a pocketknife a gentleman might own.

'Who would have thought that Tobias Freeman would own such a well-crafted piece of workmanship,' the commandant said.

Ferguson glanced up at his tone but remained silent.

'Where is Gray now? Has he finally got up off the ground?'

'I believe he's dusting off his breeches.'

'There is some dirt so deeply embedded, lieutenant, that no amount of laundering will remove it. And I'm not giving you instruction on how to scrub clothes.'

When they approached the Wheatsheaf Inn, the publican had already prepared the spread. He had set to pouring tankards of ale, and even though it hadn't gone noon, many of the men were eager to sit and talk and fill their mouths.

As disappointing as the fruitless search had been, the commandant knew that the killer still lurked amongst them. It was an unsettling thought, and he considered what to do next.

Each man carved himself a slice of mutton and took a wedge of damper. Some sat around the fire, a handful outside in the sun. Most of the men used their own pocketknives to cut their meat, but as Jim went to take his portion from the spread, the commandant noticed he had no blade, and was casting his eyes about to see where the publican had left one.

On a whim, the commandant stood and took the knife from his pocket that Ferguson had put into his hands. 'Don't you have a knife?' he asked Jim.

'Got a big one back at the cottage.'

The commandant nodded and extended the knife. 'Here, take this one.'

'Obliged, sir.' Jim cut the meat and held the knife out to the commandant when he had finished.

The commandant shook his head. 'I have one of my own, that one's yours.'

Jim looked down at the knife, then back at the commandant questioningly. Jim thought it was a handsome tool. His eyes were lit. 'Are you giving it to me, sir?'

'I am. Take it. Keep it.'

Jim admired the knife and smiled up at the commandant like a boy.

The commandant's father was a goldsmith, and fine metal craftsmanship was commonplace to the commandant, but not to the free settler in front of him who doubtless had to scrape for every crust and crumb.

'Thank you, Commandant Morisset. I've never had anything of the like.'

The commandant nodded his acceptance of Jim's gratitude

and went back to his meal.

As he did, he noted Gray's flitting expression. Sitting solitary in the corner, like a raven waits for opportunity, the officer's seeming displeasure disappeared in the blink of an eye. Replaced with a look of polite affability.

'That was a generous gift, sir. I don't know that someone like that would appreciate it.'

'On the contrary, Gray, I would be surprised if that man didn't treasure that knife many years from now.' It gave him pleasure in knowing that someone deserving of the gift was the new owner of the knife.

Gray had given himself up. The truth had been in his eyes.

Thirty

As Tobias walked along the foreshore, the wind ruffled his hair. Emma's heart raced at the sight of him. He met her gaze and smiled.

When would the killer be brought to justice? When would Tobias be exonerated? Fears circled like the crows that cawed above the township. She often saw them picking in the midden above Prospect Hill. Near the hospital they stalked like funeral directors, black coats gleaming, pallid eyes sharp. They missed nothing, neither scrap nor skerrick.

Mrs. Brown could not abide them, and when they called loudly from the treetops in early morning, the parson's wife would go out to the garden and clap her hands loudly to shoo them away.

'Black devils!' she would scold them. Parson Brown would remind his wife that they were all God's creatures.

'No man is all good, and no man is all bad. They are merely the birds the Creator meant them to be.'

Emma wondered if the same went for human beings too, but then men knew the difference between right and wrong. They had the ability to weigh the scales of good and evil. A man chose his path. So in some ways she felt sorry for the crows, maligned for their character, criticised for their song, for they couldn't help what they were.

Emma walked towards Tobias. She offered a smile of welcome, and he put his hands in hers.

'I'm glad you are home. Sooner than I expected,' Emma smiled.

'Aye? You don't complain?'

'I'm not disappointed in the slightest.'

He pulled her towards him momentarily. She felt his breath stir the tendrils of her hair. Emma closed her eyes for fleeting seconds. He let her go before gossips should see.

'We didn't catch him, the killer, you know. We found not a trace of him, whatever his name may be.'

Her dismay mirrored what she saw on his face. Emma felt the prick of tears. She feared for the future.

'Don't get upset, Emma. We both need to be strong. The person responsible will be found sooner or later, mark my words. He won't be able to hide forever.' They walked side by side in the direction of the rectory. As they walked up

Prospect Hill, Mistress McGuiness was making her way down. Disapproval lined her face.

'I see the Devil has been looking after his own,' the woman commented sourly, drab taffeta skirts winging around her as she walked.

'Aye, you and I both it would appear, Mistress McGuiness.' Emma glanced at Tobias and saw his smile, triumphant. Mistress McGuiness made a noise of the utmost disgust as they passed one another.

'Sure and isn't that the pot calling the kettle black?' Tobias shook his head as they passed.

'One day she may well apologise to you.'

'I don't need any apologies from that woman. It's you that I feel for.' Emma looked questioningly at him.

'It's not right that your name should be blackened because of me.'

'It is not by the people that know you for the man you are. What the others in the colony think is their concern. I won't let it worry me.'

Tobias might be a free man, but for many he was still a convict, even yet. Those who didn't know his past, his story or circumstance, would continue to make their own assumptions on who they thought he was.

'*We are not the sum of our past mistakes.*'

He had said it to her before. A man was made of so much more than the errors in his life. Yet she thought that if he were to face someone like the gentleman farmer again, taking a young unwilling woman's virtue as though that was his right, he would fell the man just the same. He had taken the law into his own hands, but would justice have been served if he had not? Emma knew the answer to that. There were many unwilling young women. Tobias's sister had been but one.

As they passed the gaol, its twelve-feet high walls loomed. Emma recalled her visits there with Tobias, and shuddered.

'I want you to be on your guard,' Tobias began.

Emma stopped and frowned, waiting for him to go on, searching his face for answers.

'Against what, or whom?'

'Octavius Gray,' he growled. Emma took his hand and pulled him gently around to face her. He glanced at her before looking away and into the distance.

'What happened at Wallis Plains?'

'The search party had begun, and I had just been talking to Jim. You remember the witness that told the judge I was innocent?'

'How could I forget?'

Tobias ran a hand through his hair. 'As I walked along, I looked behind me and saw Gray. He seemed to be hanging back, as though he was waiting to speak with me.'

'And was he?'

Tobias cast a sardonic smile seaward. 'More than that, he told me that when I was hanged for the crimes I had committed, that he would make sure he looked after you real good. I took offence.'

Emma shook her head. 'Tobias, please don't borrow trouble.'

'Would you have me ignore it then? When another man lays down an insult about the woman he loves, it's hard to turn the other cheek.'

'Perhaps he was goading you.'

'No perhaps about it; he *wanted* me to strike out.'

'But why did he want you to hit him? I don't understand.'

'Just in case you haven't noticed, Emma, there aren't many women in these parts, marriageable or otherwise. Perhaps you haven't seen the way Gray looks at you, but I'm not blind, and he wants me out of the way just so he can get to you. He wants nothing more than to see me gone, and is prepared to use his authority to try and make it happen.'

'So because he throws an insult, you throw a punch?'

Tobias threw his hands up in the air. 'Anyone who calls himself a man would do the same. I was protecting you, can't you see that?' Frustration and anger fought alongside one another. She heard it in the tone of his voice.

'You can't protect me behind the walls of His Majesty's gaol,' she reminded him. He looked at her and sighed.

'I know that.'

They both knew that.

'So what was the outcome?'

'The outcome was that he didn't get the commandant to believe that I tried to stab him with his own knife.'

Emma gasped.

'Aye, the scoundrel pulled the blade from his jacket and made a swipe at me, so I grappled with him and threw it to the ground. He told the commandant I made to stick him, which was nothing but a barefaced lie.'

Emma put her hands over her face.

'Could have been worse,' Tobias shrugged. 'The commandant

might have believed him and had me thrown in prison for attacking an officer of the crown. I tell you, Emma, the man's a cur.'

'I can hardly believe that anyone could be so malicious,' Emma breathed.

'I know you couldn't,' he smiled. 'Will you take heed of what I say?'

'I will, you can be certain.'

Yet although she hearkened to what Tobias had said, and gave the man a wide berth, Emma found no fault in the behaviour of Octavius Gray a few days later. Emma couldn't fail to notice the help he gave to Parson Brown in moving trestle tables in the hall in view of using them for seating after the service of the feast of Saint James.

It had been raining. The church steps were wet, and when Mrs. Brown slipped and fell heavily on the porch, it was Officer Gray who helped her up and escorted her to a nearby pew.

'Thank you,' Mrs. Brown patted his arm in appreciation.

'I fear you will have a nasty bruise, Mrs. Brown,' he commiserated.

'Indeed, young man,' she managed to smile. 'Still, I daresay I've suffered worse than this. I'm only glad you helped me rise. Once I'm down, my knees are never keen to cooperate on getting me back up.'

'And you know how the damp plays up with your aches and pains, my dear.'

'What's one more ache?' Mrs. Brown grimaced.

The parson took a worried look at his wife before he made his way to the dais, preparing the Eucharist while the congregation filed into the shelter of the house of worship.

Emma glanced at Tobias. His eyes were on Octavius Gray. The officer reciprocated the look of ill will, and Emma couldn't help but worry when she ought to have had a heart for peace.

Tobias didn't need more trouble.

Parson Brown said, 'And he saith unto them, Follow me, and I will make you fishers of men. And they immediately left the ship and their father, and followed him.' The parson looked at the congregation as one body, taking in every eye.

'They brought unto him all sick people that were taken with diverse diseases and torments and those which were possessed with devils and those which were lunatic, and those that had the palsy. And he healed them.' He smiled and paused.

'I'm here to tell you, friends, that we all have demons. We are all haunted by our past in some way or another, but often the only one who condemns us is ourselves. Men and women in the gallery,' he looked up to where the convicts sat apart.

'You have been tried, convicted and gaoled, but no man can chain your hearts unless you allow it to be so, regardless of the time you serve.'

The congregation sat in silence. When they filed out of the building, Emma's eyes were drawn to her Aunt Adelaide. She stood apart, the suffering in her heart plain as the lines on her face.

Phoebe stood beside her, but the smile she wore was strained. Emma was reluctant to walk over and greet the woman yet if she waited for her aunt to bridge the gap between the two of them, reconciliation might never happen. With the parson's words upmost in her thoughts, Emma stepped forward.

'Good morning Aunt Adelaide.' She turned to Phoebe. 'You look well.' She squeezed Phoebe's hand, taking in her pink cheeks.

'Phoebe ought to be at home,' Aunt Adelaide said, taking a quick glance down at Phoebe's burgeoning stomach before glancing away. It had increased in size rapidly.

'Perhaps, Mama,' Phoebe agreed, 'but it's hard to remain at the cottage day in, day out. I only see Rory at supper time, and

I do get sick of talking to myself.' Phoebe begged her mother to understand.

'We can only hope that the congregation will think you've put on more weight. I see now why you were in such a hurry to be wed.' Aunt Adelaide whispered.

Phoebe flushed but said nothing. Emma's curiosity was satisfied; at Phoebe's expense. She was still the cousin Emma loved and remembered, and had seen too little of lately.

Convict women could walk around in their condition for all the world to see, many hardly caring if their children were conceived in wedlock or not.

'I would like to come and visit you, when you have a mind for company,' Emma began. Phoebe's smile was the sun breaking through an opening in the clouds.

'I wish you would Emma, you and Tobias, both. Why, you could come for supper.'

'How could you?' Phoebe's mother asked.

'Whatever do you mean, Mama?'

Emma looked from one to another. She saw Phoebe quail as she waited for the onslaught, and Emma wished she had never spoken, wished that she had saved her cousin the embarrassment of walking over, but it was too late.

'However can you think to ask? You are no blue-stocking, Phoebe my girl, but I would have thought you possessed enough intelligence to realise that supping with a murderous ex-convict and some turncoat chit is not the done thing. Why, one has no more morals than a Dublin City rat, and the other was brought up to know better, yet it seems she does not.' Aunt Adelaide's look was scathing, Phoebe's stricken. 'And in your condition!' her mother hissed.

'Mama, Emma is my cousin. She is also my dear friend.'

'Aunt Adelaide, I sorrow for your loss,' Emma interjected,

'but on the day you lost your daughter Euphemie, Phoebe lost a sister, besides.'

And in the anguish of her loss, Aunt Adelaide forgot the gaunt husband and the lonely remaining daughter. Adelaide stood stonily silent. Emma didn't want to see Phoebe distressed any further, and had enough discretion to let it go.

'We are going into the hall for tea now. Come with me Phoebe, but do cover yourself a little more with that shawl, and let us hope that it veils your eagerness to have become wife to Rory Ferguson.'

Aunt Adelaide broke the brittle tension like a teacup, turning her back on Emma to walk away.

Phoebe looked back and gave her a meaningful look. 'Come by soon. We can talk further then.' Emma nodded and watched her cousin follow after her mother. All thoughts of a pleasant Sunday had been shattered.

The demons Parson Brown spoke about would not be exorcised this day.

'You wear a haunted look, Miss Colchester.'

Emma turned to find Octavius Gray standing beside her.

'I was thinking about the recent death of a family member,' Emma admitted, making to take her leave.

'Ah, that would be Miss Euphemie; my condolences to you.'

'Thank you,' Emma sighed.

'We are no closer in finding the person responsible for the act either I'm afraid, although I have my own suspicions.'

'Have you voiced them to the commandant?'

'Yes, I have, but my senior officer has his own ideas.' He chuckled. 'I believe the man has been here in command long enough. I think he's ready for sweeter pastures.'

Emma's brows rose. 'The commandant is hardly of an age to retire.'

'Not at all,' Gray agreed hastily. 'But I do think he has had an abundance of the place, and I wouldn't be surprised were he to find another nut to crack.'

'That would be a loss to this colony, but certainly a boon to another. And you, Officer Gray, do you aspire to rise to the post of commandant?' It was meant innocently enough, but the man looked uncomfortable.

'I would consider tackling it, were I handed the opportunity. It's a role that needs discipline.'

'Of oneself, or one's task?'

'The duty, of course Miss Colchester,' he answered.

But Emma wondered if Octavius Gray was more ambitious than he would have had her realise.

'I wonder if you might like to accompany me to the supper night planned at the commandant's cottage?'

'I thank you for the invitation, Officer Gray, but I must decline. I don't think that Mr. Freeman would think too well of the engagement, and I hardly think that your invitation is meant for us both?'

'I must admit, Miss Colchester, that I had hoped to have your company all to myself. Do you and the gentleman have an understanding?'

'I believe we do.'

Octavius Gray gave a look askance. 'I had been told that you were to wed Gideon Quinn?'

'Officer Quinn passed away,' Emma reminded him, even as she flushed.

'I would have thought mourning precluded you from courting.'

'We are not courting. Yet if mourning precludes me from private arrangements, then it would stop you from asking me to the commandant's supper, would it not?' Emma's smile was arch.

'Indeed, you are correct,' he said, and appeared to contemplate the shine on his boots. He looked up then.

'I distinctly recollect you saying that you believed that Gideon Quinn was not dead. You told the commandant that you thought he roamed even still.'

Emma cast him a questioning look. 'I can't remember telling you this.'

'The commandant shared it with me. He wanted my opinion, and I gave it to him.'

'May I ask your thoughts on the matter, Officer Gray?'

'Octavius, please,' he smiled, all charm. 'I told him that you were overwrought, that what you needed was sensitivity and understanding.'

'You think it's a foolish notion?'

'On the contrary, Miss Colchester, it is perfectly understandable. Only think, that if it were true, then you would still be engaged to wed Gideon Quinn.'

Emma met his eye. His features were placid, his eyes wide and innocent as a child's. Yet Emma knew that Tobias had been right about this man. He would be an adversary just as willingly as he would be her beau. Octavius Gray didn't like to be spurned.

Emma bid the man good day.

Thirty-one

Emma and Tobias sat around the fire with the reverend and his wife. It had rained all day and the glowing embers were a comfort in the manse, but her unreasoning fears concerning Gideon hadn't gone. At a knock on the door, Emma's heart skipped a beat.

Mrs Brown must have seen her panic in her face. Getting up, she was quick to reassure her. 'It's alright Emma dear, please remain seated while I answer the door.'

The three looked up at the sound of the commandant's voice. Emma turned to Tobias fearfully. Had the colony's head come to take Tobias away? This notion was not so ridiculous, and every bit as frightening.

But Commandant Morisset shook both men by the hand before he took the seat that was offered him. Had he come on a social visit? Emma wondered at the nervousness that had plagued her of late.

'I'll come right to the point,' the commandant began, sitting forward in his seat. 'Thank you, Mrs. Brown,' he smiled briefly as the woman handed him a small glass of port wine. He took a sip and raised his eyes to Emma. 'Miss Colchester, this is an awkward subject, and it involves Officer Quinn. If you would prefer to leave the room I understand.'

'He is alive?' Emma breathed, putting her hand to her mouth. The commandant shrugged.

'That's what I want to find out,' he told her. 'Are you willing to sit and listen to this?' He looked at the women in turn.

'I'll stay,' Emma nodded.

'As will I,' Mrs. Brown said.

'I want to exhume the body at Wallis Plains.'

Emma's gasp of horror was as loud as Mrs. Brown's.

'I apologise, ladies. This is not pleasant, I know. Now you understand my reticence to speak of this in your presence.' The commandant held up his hands in appeal.

'When you came to me with your doubts about Gideon Quinn's death, I must admit, I thought you were unduly anxious. But when a lady residing in Wallis Plains came to me with a complaint about her missing husband, it made me think.' The commandant sat forward in his seat. 'You see, the woman's husband is a soldier. He hasn't been seen for some two months, and as it happens, the man has been gone for around the same length of time as Officer Quinn.'

'It takes more than a red woolen coat to distinguish one body from another,' Tobias reasoned.

'Absolutely!' the reverend chimed.

'That is true. But there are some distinguishing marks that will help me to ascertain the identity of the deceased. Now, I've written to the governor stating my intention of having this exhumation carried out, but I fear that if left too long, we won't be able to find out anything at all. I don't know the rate of decay in a cadaver,' he cleared his throat. 'But being winter, and having some excellent identification markers to go by, we should be able to determine the true identity of the deceased.'

The reverend sat forward. 'And what is my part in this, since there is a parson in residence in Wallis Plains?'

'Technically that's true,' the commandant agreed, 'but it appears the man has gone far afield on parish duties and can't be expected to return any time soon.'

'I see.'

'So I would ask, Father Brown, that you would consider accompanying me and a few other officers in this endeavour, so that the proceedings are gone through with the utmost respect to the dead.'

'Of course I will be of assistance.'

'It will mean that your parochial duties here will be unattended for some days, but this is a matter of some urgency. If I get the blessing of the governor in the meantime, all well and good. I hardly think that he will forbid it.'

'When would you like to carry this out?' Parson Brown asked. 'Perhaps it will be next week. It may be the week after.'

The parson looked to Tobias. 'You will be here in my absence with my wife and Emma?'

'Aye, you can be sure of it.'

'So be it,' the reverend nodded.

The commandant addressed Emma. 'It only remains for me to ask for your consent, Miss Colchester. As Quinn's intended, you are the only one I can call next of kin.'

'You have it.' Emma nodded.

'Thank you, Miss Colchester. I will have you sign a document to that effect when I may. And once again ladies, I extend my apologies for this unsavoury visit. I only hope that my next will be under more pleasant circumstances.'

'It is a horrible thought,' Emma agreed, 'but I will be relieved to know your findings.'

Mrs. Brown patted Emma's arm. 'My thoughts go out to the woman too, whose husband is lost. Such a terrible time of uncertainty.'

'As to the search for the murderer of the two innocent women,' he said, 'we are little more advanced in the investigation than what we were before it.'

'There is no woman safe in the colony until the perpetrator is caught. That's why I'm only too glad you'll be here in my stead when I'm gone,' Parson Brown told Tobias. 'Although my strength is not as it once was, I like to believe that a servant of

God still has sway with society's depraved.'

'I wish I held your view,' Tobias shook his head, 'but I don't think a monster like that has qualms over what God thinks. For if a murderer cares not what his Maker thinks, why would he respect the sanctity of the robes of a priest?'

'I am inclined to agree with Tobias,' the commandant stood up and went to the door. 'If only it were not so, yet I fear you think too well of the world, Parson Brown. I for one, have seen too much of it, and my eye is jaded with the foul acts of men.'

'Commandant Morisset is right,' Mrs. Brown said. The parson smiled humbly and took his wife's hand and held it for a moment. 'It is no character fault in my book,' she smiled.

The commandant stood to leave. 'I'm having a supper night in a few days hence,' he told them. 'I'd be obliged, Parson Brown, if you and Mrs. Brown would come. You too, Miss Colchester, to be sure.' He glanced quickly at Tobias, who answered for him.

'Don't feel bad on my account, commandant. I might be a free man now, but I will always be a convict to some in the colony, and I hardly expect to be invited to a dinner party, especially since I was eating my tea in a cell not long since.'

'Then I must make my apologies as well,' Emma told the commandant. 'For where I go, Tobias goes.'

'I'm sorry for it,' the commandant told them regretfully, 'but society makes its rules, and I must abide by them. For what it's worth, I see you for the man you are. But as you rightly say, not so long ago you were gaoled under the suspicion of murder, tried as a criminal. And though your innocence was vouched for, there would be those at the party who would cause a scene, you may be sure. Would it be worth it?'

'No, it would not,' Tobias told him. 'I keep company with those who would call me friend.'

'I hope you consider me one.' The commandant put out a

tentative hand. Tobias shook it. The commandant nodded. 'I will wish you all a good night, then,' and he walked out into the night.

Mrs. Brown shook her head as she watched him disappear into the rain. 'You can't go out in this downpour to go to the vestry, Tobias!' Mrs. Brown closed the door on the onslaught.

'If Limeburner's Bay, convict rations, gaol tucker and a few good floggings can't kill me, I doubt the rain will,' Tobias grinned. 'Have you forgotten the rain back home so soon?'

'No, I haven't, but even still, there's a fire burning here. You shall sleep by the hearth. It will be cold as the grave in the vestry. You would be soaked to the skin by the time you got to the door of the church. Why the commandant couldn't have waited until morning, is beyond me. Now do as you're told and stay put. I'll get some bedding.' She turned to wink at Emma. 'He will have no excuse to let the fire go out now, will he my dear?'

'No, indeed,' Emma smiled.

Tobias took mock offence. 'And will milady require porridge upon waking? Oh, the impudence!' Then Tobias caught her up in his arms and they fell onto the settle.

When Mrs. Brown came out, blankets in her arms, she cloaked her amusement with a look of profound embarrassment.

'Well, I never.'

'She wrestled me and brought me down hard,' Tobias protested, laughing.

'That's enough of your shenanigans, young man, or you'll be out on your ear in the rain!'

Mrs. Brown lightly cuffed Tobias and let them see her glee. He smiled like a boy, and Emma noted Mrs. Brown's fond glance at Tobias.

'You'll be nice and warm here tonight, Tobias. Now, who's for a hot drink before bed?'

'Oh, yes please, dear,' Parson Brown said, coming back into

the room. He swung the pot over the blaze for his wife.

'I have been trying to maintain decorum, Parson Brown.' Mrs. Brown tried for a severe look, which ended as a smirk. 'These two need to say their vows before too much longer, or else I won't be responsible for the outcome.' The parson turned to his wife with a questioning look.

'Is that so?' he asked, wide-eyed.

'Who's the one talking blarney now?' Tobias laughed. Emma and Mrs. Brown joined in, and the parson was left staring at the three of them, perplexed.

'It must be later than I thought,' he muttered, checking his timepiece. 'You all appear delirious with the need for sleep. You just sit down my dear and rest your weary head,' he smiled. 'I will see to a pot of tea.'

Mrs. Brown said of a sudden, 'I don't relish the thought of seeing Adelaide at the commandant's supper.'

'Why ever not, my dear?' The parson turned from his task.

'I went to visit her just the other day, and she is sorely changed.' She looked sorrowfully at her husband.

'Why, that's understandable,' he replied.

'I know. I agree. But dear Adelaide has turned in on the world and herself in such a way that it's unnerving to sit in the same room as her.' Mrs. Brown looked up at her husband, who came over with the teapot. Tobias followed with the cups on a tray.

'My dear, you surprise me,' the parson said. 'Did you go with her, Emma my dear?' Emma opened her mouth to answer.

'Why Parson Brown, of course Emma did not go. Adelaide asked the girl to leave the house because of Tobias. Don't you recall?'

'Yes, it had slipped my mind, I confess.'

'Then perhaps it's because you're harbouring Tobias and I. That would account for her behaviour if she was churlish,' Emma suggested.

'I believe you may be right.' Mrs. Brown sighed. 'I only hope that she is in a more agreeable frame of mind if she and the doctor go to the supper. I would like to be a friend to her, but she is making it so very difficult.'

'Time,' the parson suggested. 'Give her time. They are going through what no parent ought to have to bear. Continue to think well of her, and eventually, she will thank you for remaining a friend. In the meantime,' he said, 'let us hope that the murderer is found and brought to justice.'

Outside the wind moaned. It sang eerily around the timbers of the house, as though it sought to gain entry. Emma listened to its cadence and shivered.

'Are you cold?' Tobias asked her.

'Just listening to the howl of the wind.' She was thankful for her hand in his.

'It is strange, is it not?' Mrs. Brown agreed.

'Still,' the parson looked at Emma, 'for all that it sounds human, it can't hurt us.'

'It sounds like a spirit,' Mrs. Brown whispered. Her husband frowned at her and shook his head.

'Well, I *imagine* that's what one would sound like,' she flushed.

Tobias smiled a little. 'My grandmother used to say that the dead can't hurt us, only the living.'

'Never a truer word spoken,' the parson nodded. And this was exactly what Emma feared.

Thirty-two

Adelaide hadn't felt like going to the commandant's supper. She hadn't felt the need to socialise in a very long time. She wasn't sure why this was so, perhaps it was just that the days stretched on interminably.

She took no notice of the calendar. She merely woke, ate, sat out each passing day, and waited for its conclusion.

Sometimes she would sleep on and off all day. It meant that she was wide awake at night, but then that hardly mattered, because if she sat up watching the moon until the wee hours, she could sleep in for as long as she liked.

Adelaide surveyed the menu and turned up her nose. Spiced tongue. Brains in calf's foot jelly. She could not abide the stuff, had quite enough brains of her own, and felt no inclination to dine on those of an unsuspecting bullock.

'Spiced tongue,' Adelaide said to George, 'how I loathe it.'

'No tongue can best yours, my dear,' he chuckled.

Adelaide didn't appreciate his witticism, and told him so without so much as uttering a word. George looked down at his menu.

'Still,' he said, 'there's roast saddle of mutton, not to mention plum pudding. I know you will like that, will you not?'

Adelaide nodded her head.

She knew that plum pudding was also George's favourite, but she had ceased to care. She supposed that her husband hardly knew the woman with whom he shared the cottage anymore. She had changed so much since Euphemie's passing. He began to speak and she looked up.

'Oh look dear, here is Parson and Mrs. Brown.' Adelaide sent George a withering look.

'What is that to me?'

George blinked. 'Why, Mrs. Brown is a friend of yours, is she not?'

'She was my friend, but not any longer. You seem to forget that the pair are lending their hospitality to the ex-convict and that niece of yours.'

'Tobias was not the cause of Euphemie's death, Adelaide. The witness vouched for his innocence.'

'The free settler is probably one of the cove's cronies for all you know.' George looked at her, considering her words.

Adelaide's voice was thick with scorn. 'You know, George, for someone who wears spectacles, you seem to see remarkably little.'

There was a silence between them. When George hailed the parson and his wife, Adelaide gulped on her claret cup, pretending oblivion at their presence.

'Mrs. Brown is waving to us, dear,' George remonstrated gently. Adelaide gnashed her teeth behind a closed-mouth smile and looked up.

The woman was waving that damnable handkerchief like some white flag of peace. It wouldn't work. Mrs. Brown's arm would grow tired long before Adelaide's resolve would.

She quaffed the claret and set down the empty glass. She looked around and sighed, wondering when it would be deemed acceptable to request more. George watched her silently. How dare he judge her! Damn the man.

'Well, look here,' Mrs. Brown said, picking up a place card. 'Our seats are straight across from you.'

'Well, and what a coincidence.' The gall rose in Adelaide's throat. She swallowed her spittle and wondered at the vehemence in her heart.

'Oh, husband,' Mrs. Brown exclaimed. 'There are iced oranges at the end of the meal. How I adore that fruit.'

'Do you recall the oranges we were given that had come all the way from Spain?' the parson asked his wife, speaking around a mouthful of tongue.

'Yes,' his wife chuckled. 'I bit into a segment and I thought that the thing was a living creature. They are not called blood oranges for nothing, you know.'

'I had always heard that they are a rather sour fruit,' Adelaide commented.

Bitter as gall, she thought, but it had nothing to do with citrus.

'Not at all,' Parson Brown appeared to relish the tongue. He was able to eat around the stuff and still keep his own flapping, Adelaide noted.

When would the mutton be served? The clink of silverware set her teeth on edge. Ah, here was more claret, and not a minute too soon.

She could not fault the rest of the commandant's choice of foods on the menu. Nor the way the pudding was cooked. When a pyramid of oranges was set down with great ceremony upon the table, Adelaide could smell their fragrance. She secretly enjoyed the citrus she peeled and ate.

Mrs. Brown asked, 'What do you think?' the reply Adelaide gave her was at best grudging.

'An acquired taste, I think,' even as she popped the last lift into her mouth.

Parson Brown looked up. 'I believe that oranges grow remarkably well in these southern climes. These oranges probably came from one of the farms along the Hawkesbury River.'

'Wallis Plains will doubtless prove a boon to the colony too,' George said. 'The cornfields will stretch for as many miles as can be cleared.'

'Yet I hear that the red gum and iron bark are too much for our soft English axes. The roots of the trees are the very devil to shift, so they seed around the stumps.'

'They tell me it's land equally good for grazing,' George agreed.

When the men left the ladies to smoke their pipes and drink port wine, Adelaide stood by the window and watched the moon. It hung low, round and bright as the fruit they had eaten after dinner. Mrs. Brown had stepped outside, and Adelaide breathed a sigh of relief, able to spend some quiet moments with the memory of Euphemie. It was the place in her mind she retreated to most days and sleepless nights, and she guarded it jealously, hating the intrusion of others.

She wallowed in her grief. Sometimes she stayed in the shallows. Sometimes her mourning found her up to her neck and out of her depth so that she almost hoped that she would drown. She wondered if it was the need for justice alone that stopped her wading into the harbour.

She thought of Euphemie in the dark cold ground of Prospect Hill and turned with a start to find that officer Gray had come up behind her.

'I trust you enjoyed your meal this evening, madam?' Adelaide nodded. 'Yes, I did.'

He came to stand beside her, commenting on the beauty of the evening.

'It would indeed be a lovely night, if the killer of my daughter wasn't right at this moment wandering freely around the township of Newcastle. I would see comeuppance, Officer Gray, and that Irishman hanged for the deeds of which he is guilty.'

The young officer looked at her with a keen eye. 'You suspect someone?'

'I suspect nothing, young man. I know the felon culpable, and I'm not afraid to voice it.'

'Madam, if you have knowledge of the person responsible

for such a diabolical act, you need to make the commandant aware of what you know.'

'Humph. He was given trial and then set free. What adds insult to injury is that someone whom I used to call friend thinks to see fit to harbour the criminal.'

'Parson Brown and his wife?'

Adelaide nodded. 'Who else?'

'A bitter pill to swallow indeed.'

'You may be certain of it.' Vehemence shook her words. 'All I have left is the ambition to see justice done. I only wish that the constabulary was as keen to bring the murderer to the noose, as they are to shine their parade boots so that they can see their faces in them.' She glanced down, inspecting the young soldier's boots. 'Perhaps you are no different.'

'I beg to differ, madam. I believe we are of one accord. Where the law is concerned, any miscarriage of justice must be dealt with, swiftly and without partiality. The crown should not have to feed felons that prey on innocents.'

'He has charmed my husband's niece – a chit we were good enough to take in – and now the girl has forsaken us to be with him. Living under the same roof, no less.'

'You think her honour is in jeopardy?'

'Mrs. Brown is vague at the best of times. She can't have eyes in the back of her head. Certainly they say that he's been sleeping in the vestry, but he is a little too close to my niece for comfort, if you ask me.'

'I'm inclined to agree. It's hardly a suitable arrangement.'

'Not that Emma is without assets.'

'She is certainly a very comely young woman.'

'I wasn't referring to her beauty, young man.' Adelaide frowned at the officer and saw his discomfort. 'She was betrothed to Gideon Quinn, who built her a magnificent home at Wallis

Plains. Now that his mother's life has been taken, Emma stands to gain his house, and that colonial reprobate who is nothing short of a murderer, will be free to wed her. Then they can live happily ever after in the sandstone house upon the banks of the Hunter River.'

'You think they are in cahoots? Madam I hardly think that Miss Colchester would abase herself in such a manner.'

'Not at all, Officer Gray, but the mealy-mouthed girl is making good fortune on the suffering of others.'

'But you think that the ex-convict in question killed Officer Quinn's mother so that Miss Colchester would be heiress to her fiancés estate? Opening the way for his own greed?'

'That's exactly what I think. As you say, Officer Gray, you and I are of one accord.'

'I hope you will pardon my indelicacy madam, but where did your daughter stand in all of this. Why would that fellow have done her mischief?'

'My Euphemie was no one's fool. She was the last one to speak with the felon the night that he took her life. Why, Mistress McGuiness saw them together outside her boarding house windows. I can think of no reason that she would have put herself into such a questionable situation with a man she usually never lowered herself to talk to. I think she may have found out something that she ought to have turned a blind eye to. That she didn't was the tragedy. Now the old woman is out of the way, and with no other relative to claim his estate, Emma will become quite the little heiress, and the unwitting accessory to that felon's ambitions.'

'That makes very good sense.'

'I've had quite a few months to dwell on it, Officer Gray.'

'I can't, for the life of me, understand why a young woman such as your niece, would throw her lot in with the dregs of society.'

'No more can I. But I believe it started when she had the ludicrous idea to minister to the convicts with the Good Book. It certainly didn't mean she had to socialise with them. But I couldn't stop it. Gideon was aware of the attraction between her and the Irishman, and the only thing that was going to stop the nonsense was a hasty wedding before she changed her mind and reneged on the betrothal agreement. Why, the girl gave him her consent long before she chartered a ride to New South Wales. They were writing to one another for some time before she decided to plunge in.'

'Her and Gideon were friends previously?'

'Not at all, they had never met. I knew that my sister-in-law was keen to see a couple of her marriageable daughters in wedlock, and I obliged her by vouching for Officer Quinn, who was looking to find himself a wife. The girl could have done worse than marry Gideon Quinn.'

She said, 'I don't blame Gideon for making that convict's working days misery. I would have had him toiling for me, too. Gideon knew the shenanigans between Emma and Tobias Freeman.' She ground out the words, jaw out-thrust. 'I wouldn't be surprised if there was foul play the day the bushranger Max Metcalfe and Gideon came to blows. How convenient for the convict that Gideon happened to get shot. More convenient still that Emma found herself kidnapped, only to be saved by her Irish hero, who then went on to bring Metcalfe to justice and gain a full pardon.'

'Talk about the luck of the Irish,' Gray mused.

'You may be sure. But then, Officer Gray, sometimes luck runs out.'

'It's not as if he has friends in high places.'

'You have the law on your side, young man,' Adelaide agreed. 'I think of unwitting people who have no idea of the kind of person they afford hospitality to. They give him food and a roof over his head, when the scoundrel could well steal everything in the vestry when they least expect it. I hope he does. It will serve them right.' The young man looked at her, considering.

'Never fear, madam, I will endeavour to see the truth brought to light. Miss Emma Colchester is another such innocent who deserves protection, before it's too late for her too.'

Adelaide turned with a start to see that Mrs. Brown was in the dining room. She had breezed in unnoticed. Adelaide had been so engrossed in conversation that she had forgotten all about the woman. Who knew how long she had been eavesdropping.

Still, Adelaide would say what she liked. She feared nothing from Mrs. Brown. The gentlemen filed back into the room then, and Adelaide avoided eye contact with the parson's wife.

She for one was glad she had had the conversation with the upstanding Officer Gray.

Thirty-three

Phoebe opened the door to Emma and Mrs. Brown. She took their damp shawls to drape close to the warmth of the fire and bustled them inside the cottage. It was bright with the glow from the hearth.

'I'm so happy to see you both! Goodness only knows how much I miss being in society. Mama was shocked to find me at church on Sunday in my state. I wait all day for Rory to get home from the barracks, for all that it's only a hop, skip and a jump away.'

'But your mama comes to visit, does she not?' Mrs. Brown asked as she sat herself down on the chair Phoebe pulled out for her.

'I do not see her often, Mrs. Brown. I fear I have lost her.' Phoebe took a chair and Emma saw the sadness in her face.

'She will come back to you, Phoebe, never fear,' the parson's wife said. 'She loves you. She is your mother, after all. but her hurt is so deep that at present she can't crawl away from it.'

'Soon there will be someone who will make her days brighter.' Emma tried to hearten her.

'Yes, when the stork comes with the new arrival, she will find joy in life again, I am sure.' Mrs. Brown patted Phoebe's arm.

'In the meantime, we are here to cheer your day, are we not?' Emma asked.

'Indeed, Emma. You are welcome at the manse day or night; rain, hail or shine,' Mrs. Brown assured her.

Phoebe smiled and wiped her eyes. She brightened and picked up a wedge of seed cake and began on it in contentment. She closed her eyes at the fragrance and flavour of caraway.

They passed the day in conversation and laughter. Later, they cleared the table of cups and saucers, and prepared supper.

'Rory would eat this stew every day of the week,' Phoebe said, layering potatoes, mutton and onions to the pot. 'The potatoes are meant to sink into the gravy and thicken it. That's the way the Irish enjoy it. It's certainly easy to cook.' She swung the pot close to the fire. 'If the potatoes fall apart in the cooking, well that's even better, and I'm getting so much practice in making it.' She turned to Emma and Mrs. Brown. 'You should stay for supper.'

'We too have menfolk to feed, Phoebe dear, and I fear parson would be hard pressed to find where I keep the crock of stale damper, never mind fashion himself some dinner.' The woman chuckled. 'We cannot have the parson going hungry. Why, the colony depends upon his Sunday sermons, I am sure.'

'Of course. We all do,' Phoebe agreed.

They turned at the sound of Rory Ferguson opening the door the cottage. He stood on the threshold.

'The church has been emptied,' he said, his face apologetic as he turned to Mrs. Brown.

'What do you mean?' The parson's wife asked, setting down her once more empty cup to turn and face him.

'Someone has been in and stolen every brass and bauble, candlestick and crucifix. There's nothing to be found. The place is empty save for the pews and lectern. All else is gone.'

Mrs. Brown looked from Emma to Phoebe, her eyes wide. 'My poor, dear husband; Emma, we must go.'

'Of course.' Emma stood to leave, taking the warm shawl to wrap it around her shoulders before she felt the damp sea breeze that had begun to whistle over Prospect Hill.

Mrs. Brown demanded, 'Who would do something so unthinking?'

They bowed beneath the wind, the skirts of their gowns like sails of floundering ships, and she was at a loss to guess who could possibly have a grudge against people such as Parson

Brown and his wife.

The church echoed. Emma stopped short just inside the door and stared.

'Who could be so cruel?' Mrs. Brown asked her husband. He shook his head in silent perplexity.

The stained glass saints wept from above, leaving pools of crimson upon the floor. The townspeople stood around, speaking in low tones amongst themselves.

'Do you have any idea who could have done this?' the commandant asked the parson. Parson Brown turned to face him. He looked vague as he considered the question.

'I didn't think I had any enemies, I'll admit.'

'Well, either someone has an axe to grind, or thinks the church brasses will sell for a pretty penny. Either way, they can't have gone too far.'

'I came into the church yesterday. I had papers to put away in the vestry. Nothing was amiss. Everything was in order.'

'You didn't lock the church?' one of the townspeople asked.

'No priest ever bars a house of worship from the needy. Day or night, God's house is always open.'

Emma heard her aunt's voice. 'Don't you have a lodger staying in the vestry? Or was it just town talk?'

The commandant looked from Aunt Adelaide back to Parson and Mrs. Brown.

'Tobias has been staying with us, that's true. He had been boarding with Mistress McGuiness, but it was no longer suitable accommodation. We have given him our hospitality, and he has given us two strong arms and the gift of his friendship.'

'I wasn't about to let a murderer sleep beneath my roof,' Mistress McGuiness spoke up.

The commandant turned to address the irate boarding house mistress. 'The man you are speaking of was considered innocent of the crime of murder, Mistress McGuiness. Perhaps you have forgotten?'

'Born and bred of the bog, what do you expect?'

Tobias entered the church. 'It is people like you that cause trouble, gossip and unrest Mistress McGuiness. It's little wonder you have to bolt your door at night. I would too if I had as many enemies as your forked tongue has made.'

'Commandant, I think you need look no further than Tobias Freeman for the theft of the church brasses,' Aunt Adelaide spoke up again. 'Why, the felon is here every night, and when the parson and his wife were out to supper, he had the perfect opportunity to take the very things which have been under his nose, tempting him to theft.'

'What on earth do you suppose I would have done with them?' he demanded.

'Secreted them away to sell them, no doubt,' she sneered.

'I don't even own a dwelling place. Where do you suppose I would have put them, I'd like to know?'

'I'm sure you're acquainted with underhanded company aplenty, who could stash them away for safekeeping. Then again, perhaps you're going to take them to Gideon Quinn's home at Wallis Plains until the furore dies down.'

'Oh, aye, and why would I take them there? Tell me? You seem to know more about it than I do.'

Aunt Adelaide flushed. 'You're courting my husband's niece so that you stand to gain her fiancé's house, isn't that true?'

Tobias's mouth hung ajar at the audacity of Aunt Adelaide's words. He shook his head at the insult. Emma wondered how her aunt could be so cruel.

'I understand that you lost your daughter. We many of us have lost those whom we have loved. But your accusations give you no commendation. I won't even grace your slur with a reply.

It's beneath me, madam. Ex-convict though I may be, I have enough pride in myself, and enough respect for Miss Colchester to apologise in your stead.' He turned to Emma in front of the free settlers of the colony, and said, 'Emma I am sorry you had to hear the bilge water your aunt just spewed out. I honour and respect you, as God is my witness.'

'Do you hear him, Commandant Morisset?' Aunt Adelaide shrilled.

'I heard it, madam. I believe it's called tit for tat.' The commandant turned from the disgust on the woman's face and said to the parson, 'I'll have the men on the look out, not just here, but at Wallis Plains, and Sydney. Things like this can't just go missing without a trace.' He bid the parson and his wife good day. The rest of the bystanders drifted off after him.

Rain was coming in from the sea, moving in a sheet across the water. Emma hurried to the manse with Tobias to try and beat it before it crossed their path. Kevin met them at the gate; work having finished for the day.

The bells finished tolling as the rain came in a gust. It had blown the hair across her face in seaweed strands by the time she reached the porch.

'Come inside all of you,' Mrs. Brown exclaimed, opening wide the door. 'Kevin please do not stand there sopping wet. Come in out of the squall.'

'For a well-dressed cove, you look pretty grim, Toby.' Kevin noted. Tobias stoked the embers and put on fresh kindling. The sticks ignited, crackling and setting off sparks as the smoke made a beeline for the chimney.

'The church has been ransacked, and I got the blame for stealing the brasses and doing away with them who knows where.'

'I wondered what the commotion was over by the church. Who accused you?'

'My aunt,' Emma admitted. Kevin made a noise of disgust.

'You mean the aunt who kicked you out on the street?'

'Aye, the very same one,' Tobias agreed.

'Well, Parson Brown and I know it's not true, do we not, my dear?'

'Indeed we do. Pay her no mind. I didn't,' Parson Brown told Tobias.

'Let's change the subject shall we, and talk instead about our bellies,' Mrs. Brown chuckled. 'Hot broth is hearty on a miserable day like this,' and she swung the kettle of cold broth over the flames to bubble. 'Stale bread tastes fresh when it's dipped in soup,' she added with a smile, 'and you, Kevin must stay and sup with us.'

'I'd better not, missus. Mary will be waiting.'

'But you can't go out in this weather. You'll be soaked to the skin by the time you get home.'

'Oh, all right then, just a quick bite. Then I'll have to be setting off as soon as the rain eases.'

But it was some time later before the soup and damper was finished, and the rain had abated. Kevin stood up and was ready to leave when Mary burst through the door with Katy at her side. Mrs. Brown took Katy by the hand and led her to the fire, draping a shawl around the little girl. Its fringe skimmed the floor around her bare feet.

'Kevin, what are you doing here taking tea, when I'm at home waiting for you?' she demanded.

'I was coming directly, Mary love,' Kevin apologised, pulling his cap down on his head as he made for the door.

'Aye, well so is this baby,' she railed.

'But it's not due for weeks yet!'

'I know that, and you know that, but he doesn't, and he's in a hurry.' She bent double then, and let out an exclamation as she stared down at the water that pooled around her.

'Look out, love, you're getting rainwater all over the floor,' her husband admonished.

'My waters just broke, Kevin, you brainless nowt!' Mary cried. And then to Mrs. Brown, 'I'm sorry for the mess.'

The parson's wife waved her apology away.

'There's going to be a lot more mess in this house before the night is out.' She swung around to Emma. 'Emma dear, you know where the linen is. Bring some along to the bedroom, and then put some water on to boil, please.'

'I can't give birth on your bed, missus,' Mary began to argue. But another contraction stopped her words and she groaned.

'Mary you're not going anywhere else, so do as you are bid and come with me. In this cottage, I am the law. Just ask parson.' She winked. 'And you three men, do you think you could manage to entertain Katy? Between the three of you, you might manage to concoct some supper.'

Emma turned to smile at Tobias who was sitting Katy down to table. 'How about some porridge?' He asked her.

Katy blinked, 'Can you cook it?'

'Aye, the very best for miles around,' he grinned, and as Emma left the room she saw him scan the kitchen with a bemused eye as he doubtless wondered where to start.

Thirty-four

Jim sat at the table, tankard in hand. He glanced towards the bar. The officer he'd taken an immediate dislike to, stared right back. Jim looked away and cleared his throat. He was like a bad penny, that one was, and Jim didn't trust him one little bit. Aye, the man was counterfeit for sure.

Jim had seen him try and stick the big Irishman with his jackknife, and when the burly Irishman had grabbed it from him, he had squealed like a pig.

Of all the lying, conniving jackanapes, this redcoat was someone to watch out for.

'Take a look at the redcoat at yon bar,' Jim whispered to Tam as the Scotsman eased himself onto the chair.

'Who?' Tam wanted to know, turning to gawk.

'Don't make it obvious, Tam. He'll think we're talking about him.'

'Aye, well aren't we?'

'I don't want him to know that. I don't like his look, and I've seen enough of his ways to know to be on the lookout. I wouldn't trust him as far as I could throw him, and that's not far. I reckon he wants the blade,' Jim whispered as he leaned over the table.

'I don't comprehend.' Tam pulled a face.

'The knife the commandant gave me. It was his, and I think he wants it back.'

'It's a nice piece, that's certain. A gentleman's knife I'd say.'

'That's what I thought, and I'll be holding onto it.'

'Och, aye, it would be a few weeks steady pay for men like us to afford a pocketknife like that.'

'Why are they back again, anyway?' Jim asked. Tam took a long draught and set down the tankard.

'They're going to exhume a body.'

'They're going to do what?' Jim was perplexed.

'They're going to open the coffin of the man buried up at the big house.'

'Whatever for? Isn't that place haunted enough?' Jim was horrified.

'It appears they might have buried the wrong man. Said it might not be the owner after all, but some other soldier that went missing.'

'What does it matter now?' Jim wanted to know.

'I guess it matters to the family,' he shrugged.

'So when is this going to take place?'

'First thing tomorrow, they say. I'm going to walk over and take a look. Coming with me?'

'Not on your life,' Jim vowed.

'Why not, Jimmy lad?'

'I'm not going to be anywhere near that place when they stir up some spectre. The things I've seen at that house are enough to make a man's courage run to milk. It's ghoulish to go gallivanting up there just to see if the thing takes a breath the moment they open the coffin.'

'What do you think they plan to do? Raise Lazarus from the dead?' Tam scoffed.

'You can laugh all you want to, but when the wraith wends its way to your house asking for a bed, don't come knocking on my door asking to stay the night, because my cot's not big enough for two.'

'You know, Jim, ever since you said you saw the old girl murdered, you've been nothing but a wet blanket.'

'Oh, really?'

'Aye,' Tam nodded, crossing his arms.

'Well, thank you very much. And I didn't see her being

killed. I heard it take place. That was what I said,' Jim corrected.

'Whatever,' Tam shrugged. 'I'm going to go play cards.' He picked up his tankard.

'I'll be on my way.'

Jim got up from the table. The chair dragged noisily on the floor. The commandant's trained monkey looked Jim's way, but Jim ignored him, giving a curt nod to the innkeeper in way of a goodnight.

It wasn't right that people thought to unearth the dead. Jim glanced over his shoulder. A breeze lifted the tail of his shirt and he shivered. Someone had just walked on his grave, as Tam would say. He walked a little quicker, glad that his cottage wasn't too far from the Wheatsheaf.

The place on the rise would have to be haunted. He counted off on one hand all that he had seen. The authorities were looking for one and the same person. The villain was a fiend. In all his days Jim would never forget that face. He knew the horror of it would stay with him as long as he lived.

He'd probably have nightmares again. Jim rubbed a hand over his eyes. Why couldn't they leave the dead to rest? The thing would walk Wallis Plains in hopelessness, and he would be forever dodging it in fear of its spectral powers, whatever they might be. As if a murderer in their midst wasn't enough!

Thankfully it wasn't the last night of October. Everyone knew that All Hallows Eve was when scarecrows walked and the dead crossed over into the world of the living. Jim had no intention of being pulled down into the other world. Even still, it wouldn't hurt to have a candle burning and the fire stoked to keep wandering spirits at bay.

He breathed a sigh as he reached his cottage. Pushing open the door he realised it was already ajar. He thought he had closed it properly before walking to the Wheatsheaf. Perhaps he hadn't been so careful after all. He shrugged, walking in to light a candle, looking around. The half-eaten joint of mutton on the table had gone, and he cursed.

'Dingoes! Serves me right.' He banked up the fire and prepared for bed. Jim's stomach growled. He'd have to make do with a crust of stale damper to fill his belly. But then he discovered that the scavenging dogs had taken that too. He slapped the latch across the door and fell onto his bed, vowing that he wouldn't go with Tam on the morrow, whether the Scotsman was miffed with him or not.

When dawn broke he found some oats in the crock, and set about making himself a hastily cooked porridge. He sprinkled it with a pinch of salt and stirred it about. The porridge was scalding but he was hungry.

Scraping the bowl clean, Jim went outside to dip his cup into the barrel of rainwater that collected the run off from the roof. He tapped the surface to break the ice, drinking the water slowly before taking care this time to shut the cottage door.

He was curious as to what the exhumation of a body entailed.

No one was stirring at Tam's house. There was no smell of wood-smoke, no sound from within, and Jim snickered. He hoped that Tam had a grog headache. But when he called out to the Scot, Tam appeared at the door blinking and yawning, but otherwise in good spirits. The man had the constitution of an ox. Jim gave him grudging admiration.

'What are you doing here?' Tam scratched his head, not bothering to turn away as he relieved himself, farted. Steam rose thickly from the frost-covered grass.

'I'm come to dig up a body.'

'Och, aye? You're a little keener at cock's crow than you were last night.'

'I don't know what you're taking about.'

'Get away with you lad. I wasn't that drunk,' Tam grumbled. Jim hid a grin. 'Come away inside and I'll stoke the fire. We'll have a wee cup of tea before we go.' Tam disappeared inside and Jim followed.

Jim sat himself down in the dim cottage, watching while Tam stirred up the ashes to find a few embers. He added ironbark kindling that scented the place as the smoke cloud drifted up the chimney.

'Now we'll get the lum reeking,' Tam rubbed his hands together in the chill of the hut. He got down the tea for a brew. They chatted idly while they waited for the water to boil. Tam stirred the tea leaves in, then turned the teapot around widdershins.

'For good luck,' he told him. Jim reckoned it should have been clockwise. But he said nothing, only crossed himself.

'You know Jim, I've learned to cook up a treat since Nancy passed. Never thought I'd manage to cook for myself, but I don't mind doing it at all. In fact it's something I quite enjoy.'

'If Polly ends up shacking up with me, I won't be cooking ever again.'

He told Tam about the mutton joint that had been filched, cursing dingoes, blacks and any able-bodied birds big enough and bold enough to have had a mind to creep into his cottage and steal his hard-earned grub.

As they headed towards the house on the rise that overlooked the riverbank, they talked about snigging timber through the bush and down to the river port. They exchanged stories of bad backs and earning a crust, but neither of them spoke of the cadaver that was about to see the light of day.

Jim had almost expected to find that the mansion shrouded in mist with bats circling the sky. Instead the day heralded spring. Now that the sun was up, the gentle breeze held none of the chill of winter. The parson's robes flapped bright in the early morning sun, dazzling as wind clouds against a blue sky. There was nothing to suggest the ritual was in the least macabre.

When Tam inched forward to hear the prayers of the priest, Jim found himself following suit. A couple of soldiers of the constabulary glanced at the two men, but seemed to think they were of little interest, and turned back instead to watch as the coffin was brought to rest of the long grass.

Jim took a step forward, and then closer still. The body was a limp puppet, set out on its stage of green grass. With scarlet coat and brassy buttons, the grinning face was a parody of good humour. But the cadaver didn't jump up like a dummy with strings unseen. Jim questioned whether he should be watching the spectacle at all. The sight was hollow, it was harmless, and it was humbling.

One of the redcoats undid buttons of the dead soldier. It exposed the dead man's chest, and Jim got a better view at what a body looked like, several months dead. He was reminded of his own mortality, and chafed.

'There's the ink,' the commandant pointed. 'She mentioned a tattoo over the heart. It's the skull and crossbones. There's also one finger missing, and that's enough for me.' The commandant met the eye of the parson. 'The crown will meet the cost of a headstone for the widow's husband. I only wish I didn't have to be the one to tell her the news.'

'I didn't think the young miss had married him yet?' Tam whispered. Jim looked at him and shrugged.

'Beats me.'

'But the Irishman told you that he wanted to marry her.'

Jim wanted Tam to let it drop. It was disrespectful to chat in church. It was probably just as wrong to strike up a conversation at the unearthing of a dead man. Tam was always trying to set facts in a story straight. It wasn't that Jim lacked curiosity, but the

Scotsman didn't seen to know how to talk in low tones. Tam only had a stage whisper, and the ape in the red coat whose knife he was now the proud owner of, kept glancing back at them both.

'It can't be her they're talking about. They must be speaking of some other woman,' Jim reasoned. The commandant's next words sealed it.

'So I ask you, gentlemen, where does that leave Gideon Quinn?' No one had an answer for that. Jim wondered who Gideon Quinn was, but understood then that he must have been meant to be the one in the grave. That would have made him the young woman's intended. As it was, the body belonged to someone else entirely.

So if Gideon Quinn wasn't the one in the coffin, then where was he? One thing Jim did know, and that was that if Gideon Quinn was indeed still alive, the big Irishman was going to be very disappointed, poor bloke. Jim liked him.

The big house stood at his back. He turned and eyed it. Harmless enough in the daylight. But he recalled that night, in the not so far reaches of his mind.

He remembered the redcoat. His very proper British tones cutting off the last words of the old woman at the same time as his hands cut off her last breath. And he couldn't help but put a name next to the guilty and ask himself if he was correct. Gideon Quinn?

He had seen him more than once, the trumped up lord in the worsted coat. Jim had caught him on two occasions, and he supposed there was nothing strange there, since the man was master of the house.

Nothing strange that was, save for the fact that he was a ghoulish predator who had the alibi of the grave.

Not anymore. Jim shuddered and wished then that his own cottage didn't nestle so close to the shadows of the trees.

Thirty-five

Commandant Morisset would have walked if the journey had been shorter. He wanted the exercise. Not for the sake of his physique so much as for the benefit of his mind. He mounted up and walked the animal from the Wheatsheaf towards the emerging township of Wallis Plains.

He had enjoyed this post, but there were times when the job was a downright chore. Today was such a one. There was a woman whose door he was about to knock on, to shatter any last shred of hope she had kept in her heart, and it was truly the last thing he wanted to do. He could have been cowardly. He could have asked the parson, or one of the other men to deliver the fatal blow, as it were.

Octavius Gray wouldn't bat an eyelid at the task. Yet Lieutenant Thackeray's wife deserved compassion. It was the least he could do. Especially after the bungle when she had gone to the barracks to voice her concerns, only to have Rory Ferguson forget to write it down, follow it up. There was nothing the commandant could give her but that final honour. He reined in the horse and dismounted, looking behind him. The men with the coffin on the cart weren't far behind. He could see the white robes of the parson in the distance.

He tied the horse to a cedar. Taking a moment to choose his words, he ran a hand up the rough flaky trunk of the massive tree. The budding canopy spread skyward. Spring was leaving winter in its wake, for the leaves were flushed with red, and here and there were new buds and clusters of tiny white blooms.

The timber getters were making short shrift of these kings of the forest. Only the strength of men's arms and the tang of steel decided how fast the progress. No doubt the river front of

Wallis Plains would be a bustling town one day.

He sighed and made his way to the cottage. The woman had told him she was staying with her sister. Well, she would have need of her.

'Good morning, madam,' he tried for a pleasant tone. It came out merely mournful, as well it might. He didn't need to say a word. She could tell by the apology in his eyes what he was about to tell her.

'I regret to inform you, Mrs. Thackeray, that your husband is in fact the deceased who was mistaken for an officer.'

'How could anyone have mistaken another man for my own John?' She was appalled. But her effrontery quickly turned to dismay. 'There's no one round about as looks like my John.' She spoke as though the notion was ludicrous. The commandant needed to temper his words.

'When the body was laid to rest, it had been some time before it was discovered.'

'Go on.'

'There was quite a bit of animal predation.'

'What's that?'

The commandant paused. 'Your husband had been in the river for some time. Fish are want to pick,' he finished lamely, shrugging away the words about the woman's husband as though the man had been worth nothing more than food for fish.

'Your husband and the missing officer both wore the crown scarlet, and I'm afraid it was assumed that it was the soldier whose house the body was found near. He was an officer serving at Newcastle. Your concerns had been forgotten, otherwise there would have been more inquiry into the identity of the body.' He wondered if she heard him.

'John liked fishing ... ' She started to smile at the recollection. 'He would ease off from shore in the boat and row out at any hour. Sometimes he'd be gone for hours on end. He hadn't been at the barracks, and it was a Sunday. It was a cold afternoon so he had thrown on his coat. I never watched for him, because I knew I might wait all day. Even by supper I wasn't too worried. I should have been, though. He couldn't swim.' Her face crumpled. Tears rolled slowly down the parchment of her cheeks.

'My John didn't drink, smoke or swear,' Widow Thackeray told him with some pride, 'so he wasn't drunk when he fell into the water.'

Pity, the commandant thought, imagining the man's last moments. He made a mental note about the hip flask that had been found. She didn't need to know about that.

'The constabulary will see to a burial and headstone for your husband, as befits a soldier of the crown. The parson will be here directly with your husband's remains. Once again Mrs. Thackeray, my most sincere regrets.'

He walked to the horse, knowing she watched him from the door. He breathed a sigh of relief, his duty done. The cart took the slow wide curve around the river. Its progress seemed to take forever. The horses were reined in. The coffin set down upon the grass. It was hardly fitting that the coffin be put to rest of the table in the house of the lieutenant's sister-in-law. There would be no viewing of this body. And there it sat, damp and greyed by the soil of the riverbank while the gravediggers began to turn up clods of black soil at the burial ground near the lee of the cottage.

The widow looked on, waiting with her sister, nephews and nieces of various ages. None of the brood looked alike. The commandant heard one of the men say he thought she was the strumpet who met men down any lane. But it was no business of the commandant's how she made a living.

He only wished the gravediggers would finish their toil. Still, six foot of soil took a while to unearth, and the family appeared to be in no rush. The children had begun to play, and the two women to chat in sombre tones. It was such a drawn-out burial. When they made their way back to the Wheatsheaf Arms some miles distant, he was glad to see the publican.

'You gentlemen will be staying the night, I hope?'

'I can think of nothing better than bread, meat and a warm bed.' He took the tankard of ale offered, sat down and put up a hand in greeting at Jim and the Scottish friend who sat at nearby.

'So, commandant,' the Scot began, 'we know who was in the casket, and it wasn't the fellow who owns that big house over yon, so where is he, do you suppose?'

'I am at a loss to say,' admitted the commandant.

'Jim here reckons he's the murderer.' The Scot thumbed towards Jim's direction. Jim seemed to shrink a little.

'Gideon Quinn?' the commandant asked. 'You think Quinn is the culprit? That's a very serious allegation to make.'

'Aye, but it makes sense,' the Scotsman said, hardly noticing how his friend's face flushed. Still Jim made no comment. 'He had a red coat, and he was walking around in that place like he owned it. Jim saw him walk out after murdering the old girl.'

'A red coat signifies little,' the commandant reminded the man. 'But more than that, did the killer have motive?' Jim and the Scot looked at each other and shrugged.

'What I mean to say is,' the commandant asked quietly, 'why would any man strangle his mother?'

'His mother?' The innkeeper raised a brow as he wiped the bar with a dirty linen cloth. The commandant could smell mildew.

'Aye? Is that so?' Jim asked.

The commandant nodded.

'That puts paid to that idea then, Tam,' the innkeeper said.

'Aye, Jim and I had it all worked out.' Tam was disappointed.

'I'd just like the killer caught. I don't care who solves the puzzle,' the commandant said.

Parson Brown and Octavius Gray came in from the chill. The innkeeper took a furtive glance outside at the gathering dusk, then drew the latch.

'I know one thing,' he told them all. 'Lately there has been a few attempts at theft here at the inn, and a couple have been successful.'

The commandant looked up. What now? The murders of two women, the theft of the church brass in the colony of Newcastle, and now break and entry at the Wheatsheaf? There was hardly time for parade ground duties, never mind hours to solve ongoing crimes.

'What happened?' he asked the innkeeper.

'Dead of night, through the cellar and up the stairs came the intruder. Bread and meat and liquor he took.'

The Scot harrumphed, 'Someone's hungry.'

Thirty-six

Phoebe had a backache. She had awoken in the night to the dull cramp. But she had thought that by the morning it would be gone. What she had done to injure herself so?

'Stay in bed while I get you a cup of tea.' Rory brushed his fingers over her cheek and plumped the pillows before he left the room. She lay there watching him stoke the fire then swing the kettle over to the flames to boil.

She tried to find a comfortable position in their bed. 'I'm going to go and visit mama today.'

'Do you really think you should? You know she will only scold you for going around the town in that condition.' Rory's sarcasm was tempered with a loving smile as he glanced towards her.

'Still, she is my mama, and I cannot stay home one day longer, so I'm going to venture out.'

'Sure, and why can't she come and visit you, that's what I'd like to know?'

Phoebe shrugged. She felt tears threaten.

'She doesn't love me any more.'

'Aye, she does.' He stopped his task to comfort, putting an arm around her to hold Phoebe close.

'I always felt I lived in Euphemie's shadow. Even now that she's gone, nothing has really changed.'

Rory made a disagreeable noise. 'I know I ought not to speak ill of the dead, but she would have been hard pressed to get a man to take her on. Would have been a spinster for the rest of her life. You two were like sun and shadow. You outshone her, and that's the simple truth.'

'She could do no wrong in mama's eyes. Now that Euphemie has passed over, it is like mama left along with her. She looks at me but doesn't see me. Doesn't care that I am here. She's ashamed of me because you gave me the child before you put a ring on my finger and it shows for the whole world to see. I sinned, but I still need a mother, especially now.'

'If you sinned, then so did I. Yet how can it be a sin to get a babe when we love one another the way we do? Far as I can see, the only thing wrong is the judgement that fills her heart.'

'She doesn't care for her grandchild either. Do you love the baby, Rory?' she asked hopefully.

'Aye, love, I surely do,' and he gently rubbed her stomach with infinite care. It was stretched tight as a drum. He put his head down against it, listened for a beat and smiled. His ears heard music in the sound.

'You know, soon you'll be cradling our babe in your arms, and will have all the company you could wish for.'

Phoebe smiled lovingly at her husband, and let him hold her close. 'You are so good to me, Rory.'

'Why else wouldn't I be? Sure and aren't you my wife? I have to treat you right,' he winked. Then on a serious note, 'I love you, and I'm sure our little one loves you. In fact, I don't know anyone who doesn't. Let that cheer you. Before you know it, I'll be home for supper.'

He went and made the tea, sitting it beside her as she made the laborious task of sitting up in bed. They spent a few moments together until it was time for her husband to ready himself for a day at the barracks. He pulled on buff breeches and boots and bent to kiss her cheek softly.

'Go back to sleep for a while. It will do you good. And when you wake up, the morning will appear much brighter.' His smile warmed her and Phoebe beamed back at him.

'I'm sure you're right. You usually are.'

'We Irish are fey like that.'

She giggled. Rory opened the door of the cottage and strode away, the crunch of his boots fading even as she strained to hear the sound until the last. She would miss him today. Finishing her tea she snuggled down into the bed once more and slept.

By the time she woke, the sun was much higher in the sky. Her back still ached, but it was well and truly time to rise. She waddled slowly to the crock of damper. Bread and jam would do. She had paid through the nose for Mrs. McGuiness's blackcurrant jam. The canes had been bursting with sweet tart fruit, and Phoebe had taken two pots of the coveted conserve.

But she found she had no appetite. Phoebe almost always relished her food, but this morning she pushed the jar to the back of the shelf. She would make use of the jam to bake Rory a blackcurrant tart. It would give her joy to prepare it for him. Seeing the enjoyment on his face would be morsel enough for her, even though he would happily let her eat all to the last crumb. Warmth suffused her face just thinking about a cosy supper between them.

Knowing she needed to nourish the child, regardless of flagging appetite, she sighed and cut the damper, dipping the dry bread in a sweet, hot cup of tea. It would keep her going until midday.

She sat thinking about what Rory said. Mama ought to come and visit her, yet she never did. It was time that Phoebe went to see her.

She stood uncomfortably and made her way back to the bedroom. Pulling a gown over her head, she looked down at herself in dismay. Whatever would her mama say? She supposed she would look well enough if she draped a shawl around her shoulders. Phoebe found the biggest one she had and cloaked her shame. She closed the cottage door behind her and made the tediously slow walk up the road towards Prospect Hill.

Phoebe let herself in through the garden gate and knocked on the door of the house she had once called home. Now she didn't even know if she was welcome to come visiting.

'Mama,' Phoebe called, giving the door a quick rap. There was no reply. Phoebe bit her lip, wondering whether to go in. Now she was being silly. She was hardly a stranger. She gave another knock.

'Mama, it is Phoebe. I've come to visit.' Still the house was quiet. She turned the handle and stepped over the threshold. Her mama was nowhere to be seen. Perhaps she had slept late as well.

Phoebe did her best to ignore the intermittent cramps that had not abated. If anything, since her walk up the hill, they had grown worse.

Her mother was in the bedroom, sitting down in front of the large trunk they had brought from England to New South Wales. Lying in her lap were baby things. Children's keepsakes, a pair of kid skin booties, and childish trinkets she remembered from long years before. She looked up vacantly, saw it was Phoebe, and then went back to what was nested in her lap. Phoebe managed to settle herself down on the floor beside her mother.

She picked up one of the baby boots, soft as a mother's touch. 'Are you taking these things out to give to me for the baby?' Phoebe's smile was bright, but her mother shot her a look, and took the thing from Phoebe.

'They don't belong to you. They are Euphemie's things. I can't give them away.'

'Do I have some little keepsakes somewhere?' Phoebe felt very small of a sudden.

'You were the second child. Most of the things you used were Euphemie's things.'

Phoebe said nothing. She was second. She had always come second, and she had always known it. It hadn't really affected her too much until now.

'Euphemie was such a clever baby. Even when she was only a tiny little scrap of a thing, she would get so frustrated with herself when her hands and feet couldn't manage what she wanted them to do.' Her mother smiled at the recollection, looking far into the past.

'But you! You never stopped talking. You were always off talking to someone. I was forever running after to you, wondering where you were. I always knew where Euphemie was. She would be right beside my skirts, holding on for all she was worth. And eat; Phoebe the way you could eat was quite extraordinary. You were the fattest child in the whole town. Why, I was quite embarrassed, and yet you ate only the same amount as Euphemie. I could never work it out.'

Phoebe's smile fell.

Her mother went on, 'If I didn't know better, I'd say you need to watch what you eat. You're carrying far too much weight. Still, I'm sure the town knows why you're carrying such a heavy bundle so early on.'

Phoebe looked down at her burgeoning stomach, then back up at her mother, pained.

'But Mama, it is no burden.'

Her mother said nothing, just glanced at her stomach and back up at Phoebe before she looked away.

Phoebe took a deep breath and held it, waiting until the pain went away. The babe had drummed against her stomach this morning but had stilled some. For that she was glad. Phoebe shifted uncomfortably, taking her mother's hand to rest against the tightness of her belly and looked up into her eyes.

Her mother flushed and drew her hand away. 'Phoebe, please don't be so coarse. No need to draw attention to what you've done.'

Tears sprang to Phoebe's eyes, her face burning.

'What difference does it make if our baby arrives a little sooner?'

'A little?' Her mother rolled her eyes.

Phoebe got up slowly and painfully, biting her lip to stop herself from moaning as the cramp gripped her. Her mother didn't bother to look up as Phoebe made her way to the door. Phoebe looked back. Her mother had gone back to yesteryear, when Euphemie had been alive, when the days had been young and bright. Phoebe walked out into the street, weighed down.

Mama had forgotten how Euphemie hadn't always been so pleasant. She chose not to recall how Euphemie had told the commandant that her mama had hidden contraband for Gideon Quinn. How like a Judas she had chosen disloyalty towards her parents in the anticipation that the commandant would look her way. All in the hope of twinkling dark eyes and a pair of buff breeches.

Yet her mother looked at the child conceived in love that swelled her tummy with such repugnance that Phoebe couldn't help knowing that mama was ashamed. She cradled her stomach in loving arms. Tears dropped like rain upon her belly.

'I will never be ashamed of you. I will never be,' she whispered. It was a promise, a pledge.

Another wave of pain drove her almost to her knees. She heard herself groan, and held on to the picket fence for support. She breathed in relief as the cramp passed. She had never experienced anything like this before. She was frightened. Not so much in fear for herself, but for her baby. She had to get home before she embarrassed herself further. She looked down the road in the direction of the cottage and wished she had listened to Rory. He had known best.

'Yoo-hoo, Phoebe!' Mrs. Brown was crossing the road to

meet her. Phoebe smiled, but another wave of pain overtook her, and she found herself clinging on to her friend, dragging noisily on air, surprised at the guttural sounds she heard coming from her own throat.

'Phoebe, when is the baby due to arrive?'

'I'm not sure,' Phoebe flushed. 'Not yet, I know that.'

'Babies can't tell the time, I'm afraid,' Mrs. Brown smiled. Phoebe looked at her and frowned.

'I must make the effort to get home. If I wait much longer I don't know if I'll be able to make it.'

Mrs. Brown chuckled. 'You may well be right. Here, Phoebe dear take my arm. We'll walk at just the pace you choose.'

Phoebe was so grateful to have the parson's wife walk by her side. 'Thank you, Mrs. Brown.'

'Why, dear you have nothing to thank me for.' She patted Phoebe's arm. It had never taken so long to reach her cottage.

'Now, you get yourself into bed. Here, let me help you take off your gown.'

'I can't let you see me unclothed.'

'We come into this world with nothing, and leave with nothing more. We are both as our Creator made us to be. We were born of His image, and I say you are beautiful. Now lift your arms above your head. Leave on your chemise if you like. I'll boil some water and make you a hot sweet cup of tea. You're going to need it before the day's out.'

Phoebe allowed her elderly friend to get her nightgown successfully over her head before the next contraction saw her roll onto the bed, the same low throated moan filling her lungs.

The fire was roaring up the chimney. Had Mrs. Brown stoked it?

'I've set more water on to boil and I'll be back directly.'

'Don't leave me!' Phoebe cried.

'I'll return with Emma. She was invaluable the last time we had work like this to be done,' Mrs. Brown assured her.

Phoebe thought about the work Mrs. Brown might be talking about as she took a mouthful of the tea offered to her.

'It's sweet, I know,' Mrs. Brown nodded. 'It's meant to be. You're going to need all your strength.'

Phoebe looked up, aghast. What was she referring to? Was she going to have the baby? Today?

'I'm afraid,' she whispered, clutching at the parson's wife.

'It's understandable. We are all of us frightened when we wake up in an unfamiliar room that we haven't slept in before. And every stick of furniture looks like a stranger at the foot of the bed. But when you wake up in the morning, you realise that it's nothing more than a chair to rest your weary legs.'

But Phoebe was swept away on another wave of pain.

Mrs. Brown kept her promise. Within next to no time she arrived back with Emma, who came in with fresh smelling linen on one arm, and a basin of steaming water in another.

'Emma,' Phoebe breathed. 'I'm going to have a baby.'

'That's why I'm here to help,' Emma smiled.

'I don't know what to do.'

'It will be as easy as eating cake,' Emma assured her.

'In that case, perhaps I can manage it,' Phoebe smiled weakly.

Her friend gave an encouraging smile. 'Of that I have no doubt.'

It wasn't long until there was no gap between pain and rest. No respite in her labour. Phoebe did Mrs. Brown's bidding, and found she was sitting up against more pillows than she and Rory possessed, and the heels of her feet were digging into the eiderdown quilt. She was told to push. She bore down, for the whole world as though she was at the necessary.

'Push down, Phoebe,' Mrs. Brown told her. 'That is it. Show

us the baby's head.'

Mrs. Brown took a peek beneath the sheet that was draped over Phoebe's knees. Phoebe ought to be embarrassed, but just then she didn't care any more. She was going to have her baby, and whether she liked it or not, no one could do this save her.

The searing pain was met with cheers and exclamations of triumph. 'Come on, Phoebe, one last push.'

There was a rush of warmth and blessed relief. The pain was gone and then she heard applause and praise and the cry of a child.

'You have been blessed with a wonderful girl, Phoebe.' Mrs. Brown said. She brought the baby to Phoebe and pressed child against her breast and went out to take away the soiled linen.

Phoebe looked down at her beautiful daughter. Her baby looked back at her with soulful eyes. She knew that in all her life, nothing would match this day. This achievement, this triumph was something no one could ever sully.

'Emily,' she confided to her little girl. 'Named for my cousin Emma who has been so dear.'

It was the very first of their special secrets they would share as mother and daughter, and Phoebe smiled.

Thirty-seven

Jim was exhausted. All week he had snigged wood out of the forest with Tam. They had floated the timber down river, but it had still been a haul to get it there. He would have thought old Tam would have been in worse fettle, but as usual the wiry Scotsman had kept up with him, stride for stride. If they continued to keep working like that, he'd need another nag. He supposed he'd be able to afford one, since it was no certainty that he was going to be able persuade Polly to be his wife.

The good thing about hard work was that it meant coin in the pocket and a full belly. He and Tam had bought flour from the mill. Then they had stocked up on sugar, tea and oats.

He had splashed out and bought a piece of beef. One half he had salted, where it would sit in a covered crock until it shone with the colour of a beetle's wing. With the other half he intended to make Station Jack.

The innkeeper had told him how it was done, and he thought he'd give it a try. It would stop the beef from drying out, the publican told him, and make a nice pudding. He'd wrap it in a piece of linen and take it with him on the road to keep him going until he got to Newcastle.

He had taken the flat of the axe to the meat to tenderise it. He was told to use a rolling pin but he didn't have one of those. Then he had soaked it to soften the flesh some more. A mixture of flour, salt and water made a dough, and scattering a bit of flour over the table – and a little over the floor– he kneaded and pummeled and pressed with his fingers until he had a piece of dough big enough to blanket the meat. Then he rolled it up in the dough and pinched the edges together and onto the linen it went. Jim tied up the edges, and lowered it into the simmering pot of water.

He hoped he'd done it right. He scratched his head and looked at his efforts with some doubt. The innkeeper said he had to cook it very slowly for at least three hours. If he didn't cook it long enough, the meat wouldn't cut, and the publican reckoned that the meat had to be soft enough to be ready to fall abroad with the dumpling that surrounded it. If this thing worked out, he reckoned he could manage to cook it again. He didn't need a wife. He could manage this himself. And he wouldn't need to share between two.

Who was he fooling? He wanted Polly like a good meal and a warm bed, no question about it.

It was hot in the cottage. Winter had gone, and he wished that he'd cooked out in the open as he'd done before Tam helped him figure a chimney in the modest shingle-roofed slab hut. It was too late now. He'd have to put up with the heat. In any case, he had plenty to do outside before he left for the harbour at dawn.

He took the wooden wares he hoped to sell to the storekeeper and began to load them into the cart. Perhaps he could fashion himself a rolling pin. It might come in handy. He secured his meagre load. Covered it over and tied it, so that the dew wouldn't dampen the wood.

He had rubbed the stools with mutton fat. He couldn't afford to see all his hard work come to naught. They'd look shabby covered in watermarks.

He checked on his meal slowly bubbling in the pot, and added some more liquid in case it caught while he was at the Wheatsheaf chewing the fat with Tam. He made sure that nothing was going to roll out of the fire, pushing the coals to the wall of the chimney. Then closing up the cottage, he sauntered towards the inn.

He was flush at the moment, and if he and Tam kept up their pace, he could afford to eat a little better. Maybe save himself a nest egg for when he was too old and tired to snig out timber for a living.

But after a tankard or two, Tam still hadn't turned up, and Jim wondered where he could be. By the time the sun dipped down to the horizon, Tam still hadn't shown, and Jim wondered whether the timber getting had taken its toll after all.

'Has Tam been in?' he asked the innkeeper.

'No, he hasn't. The place is as quiet as a morgue without him here.'

'I might go and check on him on my way home. You won't see me for a couple of days either. I'm heading in to Newcastle to sell a few things.'

'Drop in on your way past in the morning, and if the door's open, hail me and I'll nip out and see what you've got.'

'Thanks, I'll do that.' Jim was hopeful for possible patronage from the innkeeper. He'd certainly handed over a pretty penny to the man over time. It would be good to get a little back.

As he made his way to Tam's house, the she-oaks whispered with the breeze. The country around him became a little lonely, ominous even as the daylight faded, and Jim hastened his steps, hankering for company.

There wasn't a hint of smoke from the chimney at Tam's place. There looked to have been a fire that Tam had cooked on the afternoon before, but the tripod of sticks had been knocked over, and all that remained were the wooden ends that had burned away. Such carelessness wasn't like Tam.

The cottage door was closed. There was no sound coming from within. Jim called out, but there was no answer. He rapped on the heavy door.

'Aye?'

'It's me. Jim,' he called out, thankful that his friend was at least alive. And here he had imagined someone had wreaked havoc on the lonely settler. But Jim waited and still Tam didn't materialise.

'So are you going to open the door?' Jim was getting sick of waiting.

There was a shuffling of feet and the sound of the latch being lifted before Tam stood before him, disheveled, wary as he looked about.

'I thought you might have been at the tavern, but it looks more like you've just come off the cot.'

'I have,' Tam told him, moving aside as Jim walked in.

'Are you feeling poorly, then?'

'You could say that. I've got a headache that would split the timbers of a ship.'

'You're coming down with something.' Jim empathised.

'Aye, I came down all right. I came down hard. And when I woke up my beef had been stolen and I had a lump on my head like nothing I've ever felt.'

'You were knocked out? Who was it?'

'I wish I knew. I was looking forward to that piece of beef for supper last night.'

'Did you roast the whole piece?'

'No, and thank goodness. I've got the other bit soaking in salt, like you said you were going to do with yours.'

'So what happened? Did he hit you from behind?'

'Aye, he did, the cowardly nowt. Who knows how long I was unconscious. I suppose I ought to be grateful he didn't knock me out for all eternity. I must have taken an almighty wallop. I've been asleep on and off all day. Still, I'm a hard nut to crack. It's only a bit of meat, after all.'

'Why don't you share my tea with me? I've cooked Station Jack, and it ought to be ready since its been cooking all afternoon. I was going to take it with me on the way to Newcastle, but there'll still be plenty to take on my travels.'

'What on earth is Station Jack?'

'Wait and see,' Jim said with a flourish of his hands.

'So you're going to be cook as well as nurse maid?'

'I'm not going to nurse you, Tam. You'll be back in your own bed tonight. I don't share my cot with just anyone, you know.' Both men laughed as they went in the direction of Jim's cottage.

'You know, Jimmy my lad,' Tam patted his stomach some time later, 'if I was a mite younger, and you were a mite prettier, I'd marry you.' They laughed uproariously.

'Do you want me to check on the place while you're gone?' Tam asked.

'That would be good. Not that there's much worth stealing. Not unless you count the piece of salt beef I have there soaking in the crock. By the time I get back it'll be ready to cook.'

'I'll watch my back from now on. Some people don't care if they cane you from behind.' Tam shook his head. 'If I catch him at it next time, he'll wish he hadn't thought to stay for tea.'

'You'll be jumping at every shadow,' Jim told him. 'I know I will.'

'Not a bit of it, I'll have my wits about me, that's for sure.'

'In any case, there's a cudgel by the door you can take with you tonight if you need to use it as a weapon.'

'Aye, and I won't be afraid to use it.'

'Did you hear the innkeeper say that someone had thieved from him not so long ago? Must be the same rogue.'

'Aye, the robber wants to get a decent job– timber-cutting for instance– so that he doesn't have to steal from law-abiding citizens.'

Tam took the cudgel that Jim handed to him as he made to leave. 'What about you, Jimmy? Will you not be needing this stick yourself?'

Jim shook his head. 'I'll be leaving before dawn, and if I make a good go of it, I'll get there before nightfall.'

Tam looked unsure.

'Anyway,' Jim brandished his pocket knife, 'I have this.'

'That thing wouldn't bruise a gooseberry unless a body was right on top of you.'

'Maybe so, but scare tactics work as well as anything else.'

'Aye, I suppose so.'

Jim bid his friend goodnight and watched until he disappeared around the bend of the track. Wallis Plains had a resident thief and a murderer besides. Then again, bringing shiploads of felons to the country was going to elicit that kind of behaviour.

He took himself to bed early, yet couldn't help but listen to the noises outside his cottage. Still, the lump of beef the felon took after he bludgeoned Tam over the head would stave off hunger for a good while. He blinked, wide-eyed in the darkness as he recalled the filched joint of mutton. Perhaps dingoes hadn't raided his hut. Perhaps he had been wrong.

It seemed like he hadn't slept long at all when next he woke. But opening up the door he saw that the sky to the East was lightening. It was time to be off, before the crack.

The horse seemed surprised to find Jim there so early. He put a halter about her head and led her to the cart. She stood patiently as he hitched her up to the wagon. He took the rest of the Station Jack from the cottage and closing the door, stowed his excellent dinner behind the seat.

'Get up, Nancy.' The horse moved at the familiar command, and before long they were traveling in the spring sunshine, along the track that wound around the river.

He stopped once and led the mare down to the water to drink. By the time the sun was high in the sky, Jim unwrapped the linen that held his meal. Lunch in one hand, he held the reins in the other, and settled down to continue the journey.

Yet with a full stomach, and the warmth of the spring afternoon, Jim found the idea of a doze in the sun too great a temptation. He'd rest a while. He unhitched the horse and offered her water again. He secured her nosebag to a tree and left her to munch on hay. Then he lay down upon the grass in the shade and looked up into the blue above him. He wasn't going to rest for long.

When he woke up it was late afternoon. The sun was low and he cursed. He wouldn't get into town until nightfall. He scrambled up and untethered Nancy, hitching her up once more. Then setting off at a jingling trot, they left the place behind.

Clouds marbled the sky overhead and the bush became dim. Dusk approached, an unwelcome stranger. The bush was thick with trees. Here and there were big gums, cedars and she-oaks as far as his eye could see. The breeze above sighed through the pine-like needles, and as he negotiated massive trunks, he listened to the moan of the wind through the trees. Jim was a little spooked. At least he wasn't far from the Broad Meadow.

He noted Nancy. She lay her ears back. Her eyes rolled in her head like holeydollars, and she began to sidestep as though she would turn about if he gave her half a chance.

'Come along Nancy. Get up, girl.' He flicked the reigns a little, and she made to obey, when a movement in the scrub caught his eye. Like a scarlet flash of wings, or the red breast of a king parrot, and Nancy tossed her head and began to prance. Her eyes rolled wild as the figure came to stand directly in their path.

The red coat. It was hard to miss. Nor was it dim enough that Jim could fail to see the disfigurement on the wanderer's face. He sat stock-still and trembled no less than Nancy, from his hands down to his feet.

'I'm heading your way,' came the frighteningly familiar voice. 'Can I take a ride with you?'

Jim sat there, dumbstruck, unable to open his mouth. The stranger, who was no stranger at all, grinned as he waited for the nod to get up on the seat.

Jim figured he had two choices. The first was to attempt to run the villain down. The second was to let him climb on up. But he would only end up getting himself killed, because Nancy would do no such thing, and then the murderer would be riled for sure. If he acted the polite and neighbourly settler, then the fiend would feel no threat. Why, he was smiling now, waiting for Jim to speak. Jim nodded his head and the stranger came around to step up to the cart.

'Cat got your tongue?' the traveler asked as he set down. Jim made a sound that could have been yes. The soldier seemed content, and Jim told himself that if he looked straight ahead of him and got Nancy into a fast trot, they'd be at Newcastle in no time.

But Nancy got up and went into a canter without the asking. He didn't put her into a gallop because she would never make it into town.

He was terrified to look the man full in the face. Jim didn't know if the murderer wanted to chat. Perhaps he thought it odd that Jim didn't even have the manners to comment on the weather of the passing day. Was the officer grinning out of that mauled and horrible face? It almost seemed the fiend took some delight in it. His next words left no doubt.

'When I tell people I'm speaking tongue in cheek, they know it for a fact.' The jaunty polished voice was all plummy joviality. Jim didn't know what the man meant. He looked at the hitch hiker.

'Pardon?'

And through the obscene grin, out of the corner of one ravaged cheek, he stuck out his tongue. Jim yelled in horror and almost launched from the seat, holding on to Nancy who had now begun to gallop, frightened for her life.

The officer cawed raucously. It was obviously a party trick of his, and the pleasure he derived was so apparent, that the fiend hardly stopped his sounds of merriment, until the cart came to the edge of town.

'I'll walk from here,' he told Jim, and it was like music so profound, that Jim nearly burst into noisy tears. He gulped on night air.

Nancy was still foaming at the mouth. She lifted her tail to defecate then snorted, winded and beat. Jim sat back against the seat and felt the warmth of sweet relief.

'You might want to get yourself home and take a bath,' he heard the villain say. 'Your manure smells worse than that of your horse. Ha!' the felon cried, slapping his hand on Nancy's rump.

Jim stared straight ahead as Nancy bounded away. They left the felon in the shadows as they raced into the town. And it wasn't until they were well away from the scoundrel, that Jim realised that he had indeed soiled himself, and that the warmth that had run down into his boots was urine.

Thirty-eight

Adelaide sat in the garden, overlooking the sea. The picket fence out back that faced the harbour was merely made up of driftwood and paper bark saplings, bleached and twisted as old bones left to sand and sun. No artful design, just sticks really, like markers for the dead shoved in the ground as an afterthought. A long line of memorials for the forgotten.

She stared out at the harbour, wishing they could go home. Back to England, to civilisation, to their roots, yet she knew that they never could. Adelaide would not leave Euphemie here to rest out eternity alone. Why, who would visit her in the graveyard? Her headstone would lean as the years passed, forgotten in the wind that blew over Prospect Hill.

This place would be her resting place too. It was the sacrifice only a mother would make, and was the last thing she could ever do for Euphemie.

She heard the scrape of the garden gate at the front of the house. She sighed. She wanted to be alone. She had no inclination for visitors or conversation. A rap sounded on the cottage door. A scrape of shoes upon the porch. She discerned a whistled tune, strangely memorable, and somewhat unpleasant. Yet she couldn't quite put a finger on who it could be.

'Ah, Adelaide, my dear,' said the apparition. Adelaide gaped. 'I've come to call on Emma. Tell me she's here.'

Adelaide sat rigid, staring at Gideon in complete and utter incomprehension. 'You're dead,' she said at last.

'I assure you my dear, that I am not.'

She beheld the mangled jowl, the blinded eye – all the horror that was Gideon Quinn and now so much more – for it seemed that the ugliness within him, had somehow been turned inside out. What had been hidden from the world was now made abundantly apparent.

'What happened to you?' she breathed.

'You know, I don't rightly remember. There are holes in my memory.'

Dread was like a gag in her mouth to choke her. What if he blamed her for allowing Emma to be courted by Tobias Freeman? Certainly it wasn't Adelaide's fault – the chit had a mind of her own – but Gideon had relied on Adelaide to make sure her niece followed through with the betrothal. And Adelaide had done all she could to see it come to fruition.

The man before her had used fear to bribe Adelaide for his own ends for so many years, and just when she thought he couldn't frighten her any longer, he returned.

She wanted him dead, just like she wanted her questionable early life in London, dead and buried. Instead she was polite.

'You came to see Emma?' Her voice quavered and cracked. It was the fear. Her mouth was dry, so dry she could barely get the words from her throat. 'Emma isn't here. But if you cross the road to the manse, you'll find her there.'

'Visiting the parson and his good wife, is she?'

'Oh, no, she is currently living there.' Adelaide didn't want him under the impression that the girl would return, or else she would never be rid of the man.

She thought he might ask why Emma was no longer living with her and George, but he didn't. This was odd. She had never known him to be other than curious and calculating.

'The manse,' he said, almost to himself, as though he might have been trying to remember where it was.

'Be sure to give her my regards.' Anything to get him away. She hardly meant a word she said. Then he left without glancing at her again. He didn't utter another word, not even a farewell.

She sat there for a few minutes, hand to heart. Its sound reverberated in her head like a slamming door. Starting up, she hurried up the garden path, went inside the cottage and firmly closed and latched the door.

It was remiss of her to have left it open. She always made sure it was closed. Who knew what wily convicts might look inside and see something that took their fancy?

The cupboard was open, and she walked over to close the door, in case flies should get in and blow the meat. Where was the meat? She looked on the shelf in confusion. She was sure that she had put the rest of the joint in there the day before. And hadn't she baked an extra cob? How could she be so forgetful of the passing days that she could make such a silly mistake?

She sighed at her continued daily listlessness. She shouldn't have sent the indentured maid packing. This sort of problem would never have arisen if the girl had still been here.

Adelaide stood and stared. She had not been herself, she knew, but she hadn't realised that things had become as bad as this. Yet the more she retraced the preceding days' events, the more sure she was that there had been both meat and bread in the cupboard. She turned to stare at the door of the cottage, and it dawned then that Gideon had helped himself to luncheon on his way out the garden gate.

The horror of his face had only been bested by the shock of his presence. Her hands still shook. She teetered and found a chair. Gideon Quinn had been the bane of her life for too many years. She thought she had been rid of him, threatening her with the fear that he would unveil her promiscuous days in London.

So she had hidden his kegs of stolen rum. She had lied to save his skin so that he would keep his mouth closed on the past. She had tried to secure her husband's niece's interest in him as a desirable marriage proposal. Adelaide had honestly tried her best.

Yet she had rejoiced at his death, and there he had stood in front of her, bold as brass, brought back from the grave. She looked up and going to the door, opened it a crack. Peered left, towards the hospital, and right, down towards Mr. Tucker's store. Gingerly she walked to the gate, staring up towards the manse.

She could see Emma sitting on the porch with Mrs. Brown. Probably at their leisure drinking tea. Jealousy sat bitter on her tongue. Still, where was Gideon Quinn? Obviously he wasn't there, or else Emma would be in an outburst of grief, prone on her bed at the very thought of a far different future than the one she had hoped for. Not one spent with Tobias Freeman, that was for sure.

Anyone could see her, standing where she was. She darted behind a lavender bush, kneeling on the ground to spy through the pickets of the fence, as though her day was being spent toiling amongst the flowers. Level with the droning bees, she blinked as Mrs. Brown left the rectory in the direction of the colony store.

Adelaide made herself small. Mrs. Brown didn't even turn her head. When the woman was far down the road, Adelaide slowly straightened up, grimacing at protesting joints. She paid her bones little mind, and left the cottage, striding up the road.

'Aunt Adelaide,' Emma said, standing to smile uncertainly as Adelaide opened the gate. Her skirts brushed the shrubs on her way up the garden path. Bitter wormwood met her nostrils. She savoured it.

'Have you had any visitors?'

'Only you, aunt.'

'Is the parson at home?' Adelaide looked around.

'He's due to arrive back with the commandant today. He told Mrs. Brown they might be gone two days, perhaps more, he didn't rightly know. Did you come to speak with him about some spiritual issue?'

'Are you saying I have a problem I need to address?' Adelaide bristled.

'Not at all, I merely wondered, since you asked for him specifically.'

'Well, it doesn't matter. I know the outcome of his journey anyway.' Adelaide knew that she ought to have been ashamed to think it, but the look of dread on the girl's face was priceless.

She cast her net and watched it fall. 'You cannot marry Tobias Freeman.'

First doubt, and then every terrible emotion rippled over Emma's features. It was the worst news. Adelaide saw the girl struggle to free herself from the terrible fear that caught her.

'I beg your pardon?' The hopeful smile was gone. It seemed to slide right off her face.

'You aren't free to marry anyone,' Adelaide told her. Emma said nothing. Adelaide was impatient. 'Aren't you going to ask me why?'

'I believe I know the answer to that. But I'll wait until you tell me.'

Adelaide realised she was smiling. Openly smiling like she hadn't done for months.

'Gideon Quinn is alive.'

To the girl's credit, she neither fainted nor cried. She did not fall to the porch in despair. But Adelaide saw the dread on her face. She found grim satisfaction in that.

'I see,' was all she said.

'You'll have to marry him,' Adelaide bullied. 'You are his intended, after all.'

'I believe I will make my own decisions.'

'Well, Gideon Quinn was at our cottage no more than an hour past, and the only person he wants to see is you.' She saw the girl quail.

'Then he will be disappointed. I have no intention of marrying him.'

'You tell him that,' Adelaide snorted.

'I had been informed that Gideon Quinn was an upstanding officer of the crown, a young man worthy of my attentions. I was misinformed of the man's true age, but far more than that, I was deluded as to his character. I had plighted my troth to a liar and a thief, a person of questionable appeal at best. But then I learned more of him, and I knew that there was nothing that could induce me to change my mind concerning him. I cannot walk down the aisle with a man whom I neither esteem, nor care for. I don't care what society thinks. I certainly don't care what you think.' Emma gave her defiance.

'Don't give me that.' Adelaide scoffed.

'I don't know why you were never honest with me, and nor do I know why you never told my mama how old Gideon was when she asked you. I don't know what your motives were yet what I do know is that it was nothing more than a self-serving scheme at my expense. I'm not prepared to pay the price for you.'

'How dare you!' Adelaide darted forward and slapped Emma hard across the cheek. Emma didn't retaliate. She touched her face. It flamed. She looked at Adelaide.

'I see that I have hit close to the bone. Still, your secrets are on your own conscience. I have sins enough of my own without acting confessor to yours.'

Adelaide shook in the gale of her anger. She flung her glance toward the road to see that the rector and his wife were trudging back to the manse. As they approached, he looked up to where she and Emma stood. His face was grim. He knew the worst, but if he thought he was the bringer of bad tidings, he was wrong, because the girl had already been educated on the true state of affairs.

Still, Emma had turned on her in a way she had thought she

never would. Once again Adelaide was open to Gideon's threats. If he didn't get her help to secure the chit's hand, then the whole colony might learn that once upon a time, the men of London had paid for Adelaide's attentions, and that Gideon had been her master through it all. There was nothing and no one to whom she could turn.

'Adelaide,' Mrs. Brown said. 'It is good to see you're out visiting again.'

Parson Brown bid Adelaide good day and turned to Emma, taking hold of her hands.

'Emma, I'm sorry to be the bearer of bad tidings. There's no kind way to tell you this.' He sighed. 'The man who was in the grave was not Gideon Quinn.'

'You're sorry? The girl was prepared to wed him not so many months ago. As far as the colony is concerned, he's her betrothed. Yet the girl learns he's alive, only to have spurned him for another beau, and you tell her you're sorry? You may as well say, I'm sorry he didn't die, Emma, you have a sad dilemma on your hands. Too much choice is a terrible thing, is it not, Emma?'

None of them spoke. They looked at Adelaide, embarrassed. 'Truth hurts,' she spat, walking out the gate.

A familiar voice called out as she strode homeward. It was Mistress McGuiness waving from the boarding house porch. Adelaide made a beeline for the woman. She was one of the few who hadn't been duped by the Irish felon. There were not many in the colony, she thought bitterly.

'My dear, what wonderful news for you,' Mrs. McGuinness said. Adelaide squinted at the woman over the fence.

'I wouldn't say that,' Adelaide returned.

Mistress McGuiness seemed taken aback. 'I am surprised.'

'Don't be, Mistress McGuiness. There is no love lost between her and I.'

'I know it's been hard for you dear, but don't you think you should let bygones be bygones?'

'No, I'm afraid I do not. There are some things that cannot be forgotten, never mind forgiven.'

'How does the doctor view it all?'

'He doesn't know,' Adelaide told her, 'but you can be sure I'll tell him the news as soon as he returns from the hospital. He'll be just as shocked as me,' Adelaide told her.

Mistress McGuiness frowned.

'It will be a wonder if he doesn't know already. It's all over the colony.'

'Really?' Adelaide was a little shocked. 'I thought I was the first to know. I only just went to tell Emma then. She wasn't too happy, I can tell you.'

Mistress McGuiness shook her head. 'That is a shame. She ought to be so pleased.'

'That's exactly what I think.'

'Her time will come.'

Adelaide looked out to the horizon and nodded. 'Indeed it will, as it does to us all, Mistress McGuiness,' she said turning away on a sigh, bidding the woman goodbye.

She made sure to latch the cottage door. If anyone knocked, she was not at home. Although she tried not to worry about the return of Gideon Quinn, it made no difference. Let him do his worst. If Euphemie's death hadn't killed her, she didn't suppose the ghost of her past would either. Yet although she was still floundering by the time George had arrived home from the hospice, Adelaide had stirred herself sufficiently to prepare supper.

She heard his hurried steps, his impatient knock at the door. She opened it to see his beaming face. Something she had not seen for some time.

'What news!' he smiled, pulling her into his arms. Adelaide

pulled back, staring hard at him.

'You're happy about it?' she asked blankly.

'I'm ecstatic, my dear. This is a new beginning. Some brightness to cheer the sadness of our days.'

'We cannot be talking of the same thing.' Adelaide shook her head. 'What is so wonderful that you hold me in your arms like this? As though every horrible word from my lips never was?'

'Because we have been given a gift.'

'And what gift is that, I'd like to know?'

'A baby, Adelaide! Phoebe has given birth to a daughter. And it is like the sun has come out from the clouds.'

Adelaide stared at her husband, repeating his words. 'A baby? She had the baby?'

He nodded, squeezing her to him as though he would never let her go.

She wondered why if the sun was out, tears were raining down her cheeks? They fell in torrents, and she found that she was crying and laughing as though the walls of a dam had been pulled down. As though the tide was rushing in with one joyous gush and was taking her along with it. But she was in no fear of drowning. Not at this moment, not at all.

'It's all right, Adelaide, my dear,' she heard George's soothing voice, amidst the waves that carried her and held her afloat. 'It's going to be all right.'

Thirty-nine

'He cannot make you marry him, Emma.' Tobias clasped her hand. 'He's hardly going to come here to the rectory and demand parson join you together in holy matrimony. Parson Brown is a gentle man, but not a weak one. Is that what you're afraid of?'

'I know that I'm afraid of Gideon.'

'You know I'd never let him harm you.'

'He killed that young convict. How can you forget?'

'Allan, aye, stoved his head in right before my very eyes, but that doesn't make him one of Satan's legion, just means he thinks lightly of indentured men and women.' Tobias turned to Emma.

'It's a wonder the commandant never came to me concerning what I knew about Allan Campbell. Like, ask me where the body was so that they could verify my story. I suppose he didn't think I'd murdered him, or otherwise he would have been banging down the door long since.'

It was the way Emma looked at him. The way that her eyes said she was sorry before she dipped her head to the hands in her lap. It was those things that gave which gave him pause for thought.

'You did tell him, didn't you?'

Emma shook her head. 'No Tobias, I didn't. You told me to, I know, but I thought if I did, there was no one who could back you up, no witness to say that it was so. I was afraid that it would give the constabulary all the more reason to hang you.'

He frowned at her. 'He's alive and wandering the streets when he should have been made accountable long before now for his crime.'

'Yet would the commandant have taken your word against that of Gideon Quinn? Don't you understand why I feared to tell him?'

'Aye, of course I know what you're saying, but there's a man buried out there, forgotten, without a name to his grave, and he deserves justice, amounting to something more than the dirty little secret buried on Quinn's land.'

'You know that Gideon would only blame you, Tobias. You know how he'd love to see you hang.'

'Aye, and Octavius Gray would be right beside him, cheering him on, doubtless bearing witness to my every crime. I've been made free Emma, and I don't intend to live with my tail between my legs, so that every time the constabulary looks around for someone to blame, I'm huddling in some corner. I won't live my life in fear. I've atoned for my sins. There is no blood on these hands. I have been washed clean, and I stand unafraid.'

'I kept my mouth shut out of the fear of losing you,' Emma whispered.

He pulled her to him. 'This new country will be the home of our children. It is up to us to teach them to walk with heads held high, never to be afraid to speak up for what's right and good.'

'Our children, Tobias?' Emma smiled. He put a finger under her chin and brought her around to face him.

'Aye, yours and mine. Do you think I'm going to let Rory Ferguson get away with fathering himself a household full of babies before I can catch up?'

Emma giggled.

'Emma I love you, and I think we've waited long enough. I don't care for Quinn's opinion, or for anyone else's who cannot see the love in our eyes for what it is. I want you to marry me, just as soon as the parson can pull on his surplice. Will you be my wife for the rest of our lives?'

'Yes,' Emma whispered, 'I will. For all eternity if that may be.'

He thought of the fine gold band he had kept for months

with treasured hopes. The money and the band were still under his bedding. They were the only things the thief hadn't seen when he had stolen all from the vestry and church.

'Tomorrow I will go and see the commandant personally, as I ought to have done before, and tell him about Allan Campbell's demise.'

Emma nodded, and he saw the worry in her eyes. He held fast to her as they sat in the silence of the warm spring evening. It was far from curfew, but it had been a trying day. Parson and Mrs. Brown had already retired to bed.

'Go and get some sleep,' he told her. 'We'll tell everyone our good news tomorrow. Oh, and latch the door when I leave, don't forget,' he told her. 'So I'll sleep sound tonight knowing you are safe.'

'You may be sure of it.'

He gave her one last longing look before turning away, stopped at the step and looked back.

'Tonight the commandant usually plays cards at the public house. I'm going to go and reveal all to him if he's there. Then my conscience will be clear.' She said nothing, and he knew she was afraid for him; for them. 'I love you, Emma.'

'I love you too, Tobias,' and although he couldn't see the love on her face, he could hear it in her voice. He was buoyed by Emma's promise and the vow they would make. He was still smiling as he made his way into the inn.

The place was almost empty. A couple of free settlers sat in one corner, and in the other was a man familiar to Tobias, though he couldn't for a moment work out why. The man met his glance, then held up a hand in greeting, and Tobias realised it was the one who had borne witness to his innocence.

The man who had saved his life.

Tobias walked over to him with a greeting. They shook hands. 'It's Jim, isn't it?'

Jim grinned and nodded. 'Yours is the first friendly face I've seen since I got here.'

'Aye, you have a friend in me. For a lifetime, I'd reckon. Sit down again man, and let me buy you a drink.' The publican served Tobias and he came back, asking, 'What brings you into Newcastle?' Jim rolled his eyes and shook his head.

'A money-making quest that turned into a nightmare,' Jim told him.

'What happened?' Tobias frowned. Jim put his head in his hands. Tobias saw his shoulders slump. Jim looked up and sighed.

'I've been making some pieces of furniture. Just little objects: chairs, stools, that kind of thing. I had the idea that if I brought them into town, I could take them to Tucker's store and he would give me something for them to sell in his shop.'

'Aye,' Tobias prompted.

'It was heavy dusk by the time I got to the Broad Meadow, but my mare wouldn't move. Her eyes were rolling about in her head, she was that scared. That area is thick with trees, and I couldn't make her go forward, no matter how I tried to coax her. Then the reason for it jumps out of the bushes asking for a ride into Newcastle.'

'A man?'

'Not just any man,' Jim breathed, looking about him as his voice dropped. 'It was the one who killed the old girl at the big house, the fiend who squeezed the life out of her and probably that other girl besides. I think his name's Gideon Quinn.'

Tobias knocked over his drink. His chest was marching like an army drum. 'How do you know Gideon Quinn?' Tobias asked.

'I've seen his face more times than I've seen you. I was there when they dug up the body. They thought it might have been him, but instead it was some other officer – can't remember who – but Gideon Quinn's not dead, and to make it worse, I gave him a lift into town.'

'Why did you do that?' Tobias swallowed unease. The innkeeper had come over to wipe up the spill. Talk stopped until he had gone.

'Because I'm a coward, that's why.' Jim threw up his arms. 'I'm disgusted at myself. The cart was at a standstill. I couldn't go forward and it was too tight to turn. If I said no he would have jumped the dray, so I did the only thing I could do. To make it worse, most of what Mr. Tucker gave me for the furniture was used up buying a new pair of breeches.'

'Well, if you needed them ... ' Tobias shrugged.

'After the fright I got from Gideon Quinn I did.' Jim flushed. 'Scared senseless is probably the most delicate way to put it,' Jim admitted, his cheeks colouring even in the candle glow.

'Where is he now?'

'Now? Well, that's anybody's business. I would have left this cursed place this morning except that when I went to see the commandant, he was out on some errand. I wasn't about to leave it to that circus ape that tried to stick you with his hat pin.'

'I wouldn't trust him with any important information like that. He'd keep his mouth shut just to spite me.'

'Especially since the commandant gave me this.' He took something out of his vest pocket and Tobias saw it was a knife.

'Nice knife,' Tobias picked it up to study it.

'Do you want it back?' Jim asked. Tobias looked at him blankly.

'It's not mine. I've never owned anything so grand as that.'

Jim grinned and stabbed his finger in the air in satisfaction. 'I know that, and so did the commandant. He gave it to me right in front of Octavius whatever his name is. If looks could have killed, I wouldn't be sitting here to tell you the story.'

'If it's any consolation, you're not the only one he doesn't take a shine to.'

'I guessed you weren't one of his favourites,' Jim laughed. 'So now you know why I'm still waiting around here. I only hope I can see the commandant tomorrow, because I want to get back home. All I want to tell him is that there's a murderer on the loose that looks like he had morning tea with a Port Jackson shark, and I'm sure it must be Gideon Quinn.'

'But that would mean he murdered his mother, because she's the one you heard him strangling, you know.' Tobias frowned. He was sceptical. 'Wait a minute,' Tobias tried to recall something that he had heard said.

He thought back to the time when Cecily Quinn had arrived, rouged and powdered, looking as much a part of London as he could ever imagine. Tobias looked at Jim in dawning understanding.

'Tell the commandant when his mother arrived off the ship from England she never got to see Quinn because he was supposedly already dead. But more than that, Jim,' Tobias smiled grimly. 'Cecily Quinn hadn't seen her son for many years. When I took her to Wallis Plains so that she could see where he was buried, she might have realised it was him when he had his hands around her throat, but he wouldn't have had any idea that it was his mother he was throttling. He would hardly have expected to see his mother again.' Tobias sat back in the chair.

'Tomorrow morning I'll meet you and we'll go together to the barracks. Because you see, I witnessed another of Quinn's crimes, and I'm still here to tell the tale. Gideon Quinn took the head of a spade to an innocent man with his whole life ahead of him. Then he ordered me to dig the man's grave under threat that he would blame the murder on me. So you see it's not the first time that I've been accused for his wrong doing. Time to see the guilty made accountable.'

They shook hands on it. Tobias sat back and enjoyed the

company of this new friend, but he wondered uneasily where Quinn was, glad that Emma had promised to lock the door for the night.

Forty

The candle smoked and flickered. The wick ought to have been trimmed. Its long sinuous flame swayed like a dancer, the small dark plume of smoke reaching up to disappear towards the gloom of the ceiling. The tallow had sunk into the candle holder. There wasn't a lot of light remaining and soon it would sputter and die.

Emma yawned, stretching as she thought of Tobias. A smile played about her lips as she imagined their days together as husband and wife.

She had charted a ride to Australia on a promise and a prayer, and her hopes had been answered in a way she could never have imagined.

But where was Gideon? The idea was unsettling. More than that, it was frightening. But she was calmed by the fact that she was safe in the manse with Parson and Mrs. Brown, the friends who had opened their home and their lives when there had been nowhere else to go. They had done it unreservedly. She would always be indebted to them. When she and Tobias found a home of their own, she hoped they would often visit them.

Where they settled wasn't important. They would be together, and that was all that mattered. The rest was of little consequence. Were it a broken down cottage of wattle and daub and little else, they would make it their own. As long as there was love to keep one another warm, a pail could always be found to catch the drips from a leaky roof.

Had Tobias spoken to the commandant? Would his evidence be taken seriously enough to take the matter of Allan Campbell further? If only Gideon realised the trouble that Tobias was raking up.

Commandant Morisset was a fair man. Surely he would trust

in what Tobias told him concerning Allan Campbell's untimely end, and follow the matter up. Yet Gideon would be a dangerous adversary. Especially if faced with the hangman's noose.

The candle flickered and spat. A moth flew into the fat and it floundered. Dust from its wings marbled a signature in gold as it flapped fitfully.

There was movement at the open shutters. But it was not a moth. A face appeared. The ghost of a face, yet it was no ghost at all. Gideon leered in at her. Yet the countenance that stared at her had changed so much. Perhaps it was some convict hiding from curfew? Running from the law? But as she stared back at the man, transfixed, she knew she wasn't wrong. Gideon had returned and she had known it all along.

Surely he wasn't considering hoisting himself up through the frame of the window?

'Emma,' he breathed, his gums drawing back as he bared his teeth in a smile.

'Gideon? Is it you?'

'Are you surprised?'

'Indeed, yes, I am.' Emma clutched the covers closer. She sat upright in bed, rigid. 'It's late now Gideon. Curfew has sounded. The bells tolled not long ago.'

'I'm not tired,' he said, making to shinny up the wall and into her room.

'Gideon you can't come in here. I am readied for bed. Please, tomorrow would be a better time.'

When Tobias is by my side.

'I need comfort,' he cajoled. Emma gaped.

'Comfort?'

She saw by the candle's light that he was blind in one eye, and that side of his face had been almost torn apart. Then she recalled how the gun had discharged during his scuffle with the bushranger

Max Metcalfe so many months ago. The damage the gun had done had ravaged him. How had he managed to stay alive?

'I think you'd better come back in the morning.'

'My mother is dead.'

'I'm sorry to hear that, Gideon.'

'She should have told me who she was.'

A lump caught in Emma's throat.

'I just thought she was some whore in our house. Preening herself in the mirror, she was. Paint on her face, bodice pulled low. And I was reminded of all those men from the streets. It made me wild. Women like that never change. They think a come-hither smile and red ribbons is all it takes to get my attention. There was the chit on the corner, waiting for the commandant like some common baggage, but I took the stuffing out of her.'

He sat in the window. A gargoyle crouched in the candlelight. She was drawn in sickening fascination. What had that bullet done to him, and where had it lodged? Had some starburst of metal shot up into his head, killing any humanity inside of him, to leave a perverted killer without qualm or conscience?

He jumped off the sill, and into the room. She could smell him, and he was rank. He was wild-eyed and way beyond reason. He unbuttoned his scarlet jacket and she was hit by the miasma.

'What are you doing, Gideon?' Alarm rang against her ribcage as her feet touched the floor.

'Why, my dear, I'm getting into bed.' He began to unbutton his breeches, his intent apparent. He hardly tried to veil his urgency.

'Parson and Mrs. Brown will be here in any instant.'

He waved away her warning. 'They will hear nothing. They are as old as me, and deaf.'

Another button was undone, and the once buff breeches were peeled away. What had happened to this man? Had all reason been blown away? Emma lurched forward and headed for the door.

Then she was in the parlour, stumbling blindly in the dark. Soon he would be upon her, drawing her back. Would he throttle her too? She fell over her nightgown and hit the floor. It was rent at the yoke, torn to the breast. She grasped at the fabric and held tight with a fist. She pulled herself up to lift the latch.

'Tobias!' She looked wildly towards the church, but her voice met the stillness. The hush of the waves, the call of an owl. The smell of loneliness in the night, its touch upon her cheeks. And above her racing heart, Gideon was somewhere in the darkness.

The garden gate swung back on its hinges. A torturous whine, it stopped her dead. Emma veered around and glimpsed the flash of a fleshless body, luminous beneath the moon. She grabbed the cold iron handle of the church door.

'Tobias!'

Her voice was loud in the silence beneath the dark vault of the roof. Her breath was ragged in the stillness. She clamped a hand over her mouth and groped for the vestry in stumbling fear.

A noise behind her, and she spun wildly. Emma was grabbed and another larger hand was clapped over her mouth. She fought for air. Dragged down behind a pew, she was weightless with dread.

'Hush,' came the familiar voice, and Emma slumped weakly against the arms of Tobias.

Her head came up at the sound of the door. It opened a crack. Like the creak of old bones. Pale as plaster, Gideon stood beneath the archway. Then the door shut and she saw him no more. A stealthy shadow, he moved around the church, seeking her out. Icy perspiration dripped down her back.

'Creep, creep, little mouse, you cannot hide inside God's house.'

Fear held her. Tobias held her tighter. His kiss warmed the

top of her head. Encouraging her for silence, he covered her ears and held her firm against his chest. Then he was taking her hand to lead her to the door and to safety. But she stumbled over the ragged nightgown that dipped to her toes and Gideon intercepted their escape. They pulled up short and Tobias pushed her away and she fled up the flight of stairs to the convicts' gallery.

'There's no one to save you, Emma,' Gideon laughed.

'No one but me, that is.'

'Now there's a familiar voice. The potato farmer, if I recall. The bog boy, is it not?'

Gideon was jovial. That was dangerous, she knew.

'You can call me whatever you like. It makes no difference to me.'

'I'm afraid to slight you, boy, but I don't associate with people in your class.'

'Oh, aye? And this coming from a cold-blooded killer?'

'Some people deserve life more than others,' Gideon said lightly.

'If that's the case, you won't be complaining when the executioner puts the noose over your head.'

'I'm an officer of the crown. Step aside. I'd like a warmer shade of welcome from my betrothed.'

'She's not yours!' Tobias barred the way.

But Gideon drew closer. She heard him near the stairs. 'We shall see.'

Feet pounded towards her. The two men collided, falling against the banister. Gideon clawed free and made a rush towards her, and with him Tobias. They rolled and roared and she was wrapped in the reek of rank wool as Gideon pulled her away from the wall.

'No. No!'

'You belong to me.'

'No, Gideon, I don't belong to anyone!'

'Certainly not to you,' Tobias pried Gideon away, and in the gloom she watched them struggle. It was not two men fighting for the one woman. It was two men fighting for life. A fight that had been a long time coming, from the moment Emma had landed on Newcastle's shore.

They growled like animals, guttural and wild. They rolled and tore at one another. The sound of fists hitting flesh, over and over, before the loud split of the handrail as it cracked and broke.

And then a sickening single thud before the silence.

'Tobias!' Emma groped her way to the balustrade and felt a body at her feet. 'Aye,' she heard him say, his laboured breathing loud in the stillness of the dark and empty church. Emma reached out and put her arms around him.

He panted, spent. His shirt was wet with sweat. She kissed his lips and tasted blood.

'You're bleeding.'

'Aye, but not like Quinn is. Still, damnation lasts an eternity. And that's a very long time.'

Emma clung to Tobias as they made their way down the staircase. 'What do we do?' Emma turned towards the pale shape on the floor in the darkness.

'I'll go and see the commandant first thing, so that the body can be taken away. Quinn won't be going too far between now and then.' He led her away from the sight.

'You can't sleep in here tonight. Please don't remain in here with him. Stay close to me tonight,' Emma heard the pleading in her voice.

'I'll lay at the foot of your bed.'

'What will Mrs. Brown say when she gets out of bed in the morning, to find you in my room?'

'She will know I was doing nothing more than protecting

your honour and your life,' his voice low and serious now. Emma turned to him and threw her arms around his neck.

'And she would be right,' she whispered, the tears falling down her cheeks. Tears fierce and hot. Tobias said nothing, merely held her tight.

✠

Emma stood in front of Mrs. Brown.

The woman gave a satisfied smile. 'You have no need of frills and lace.'

Emma hugged Mrs Brown. 'Thank you. I'm ready now.' In truth, she had been ready for the longest time.

'But my dear you aren't even late. Why you're right on time.'

'I have waited as many months for this as it takes for a ship to sail home. I won't delay it a moment any longer. I'm going to enjoy it like nothing I've ever done before.' Emma looked over her shoulder to smile.

Mrs. Brown followed after her, and the two women made their way out of the cottage and through the garden.

The whole township appeared to be in the church. And at the dais, turned and ready to greet her, was Tobias.

The parson told the congregation, 'And Ruth said, Entreat me not to leave thee, or to return from following after thee: for whither thou goest, I will go; and where thou lodgest, I will lodge: thy people shall be my people, and thy God my God.'

Wasn't it true? Her place was with the man at her side, and this township overlooking Prospect Hill had become their home. England was leagues distant. With Tobias she would grow old.

After the ceremony, Emma looked up to see her uncle and aunt approach. Phoebe and Rory came with them. Her aunt was cradling the new baby in her arms.

'Will you accept my congratulations?' Aunt Adelaide asked.

'Of course we will Aunt Adelaide,' Emma smiled.

'Apparently I was wrong concerning you, young man,' her aunt addressed Tobias. 'I offer you my apology, if you will take that as well.'

Her aunt had admitted defeat. She had been wrong, and although the words sounded grudging, they had been given.

'I will,' Tobias assured her. 'Gideon Quinn waits for death in the hospital bed. I only hope he lives long enough to hear his trial.'

'Humph,' Aunt Adelaide said. 'I don't know why they don't just string him up without one. That man has lived too long.'

Aunt Adelaide looked down at the baby and smiled, reminded of the new life in her arms. 'This is Emily Euphemie Ferguson. She was named after her aunt, you know.'

Emma and Phoebe shared a smile.

'She is every bit as beautiful as her mother,' Emma agreed, and it was nothing but the truth.

'Yes, she is just like Phoebe,' Aunt Adelaide said. She never took her eyes from her granddaughter. Emma looked over her aunt's head at Phoebe. Saw how her cousin beamed. It seemed that the sun had come out, and Emily Euphemie Ferguson had no idea that she was the cause of it all.

As Emma looked over towards the commandant, she saw Katy dance up to him. Katy drew him with her to point under the church building. He followed and bent down to see.

'Congratulations, Katy,' she heard him say, and he approached. 'It seems the church brasses have been found, Parson Brown,' the commandant smiled.

'They have? Where were they?'

'They were under the church the whole time. Katy here was playing where she ought not to have been, and she spied them lying in a pile. Officer Gray,' he beckoned. The soldier walked over to where they all stood. 'The church brasses were hidden beneath the church. Would you crawl under there later and haul them out?'

'Yes, sir,' Officer Gray nodded. Yet there wasn't the flicker of a smile on his face as he walked away, or even an ounce of surprise.

Emma and Tobias stood arm in arm, and Katy twirled about before them. Her plait flew out behind her, bright in the morning sun. She stopped beside the commandant, and he drew something out of his pocket and presented it to her. A smile lit Katy's face and her laughter chimed like a bell.

And a man, who was esteemed above many, bestowed a most extraordinary gift to the daughter of a common convict. For as the commandant let go of the end of the braid in his hands, Emma saw it was a red ribbon that he had drawn up in her hair to tie into a bow.

Then Katy did what Emma knew she would. She looked up at Commandant Morisset, and smiled.

Glossary

Adam and Eve it?: Cockney Rhyming slang for 'believe it.'

Awabakal: An aboriginal hunter-fisher-gatherer tribe in Australia that incorporates the New South Wales regions of what are now known as Newcastle and Lake Macquarie. The Awabakal tribe, pre-colonisation, subsisted largely on molluscs and fish. Specifically, the area of what is now known as Stockton (and once known as Limeburners' Bay) was found to have huge mounds of discarded oyster shells, which had fed the people in this area over many generations. Consequently, these oyster shells were burned by the convicts to make lime.

Bloke: Slang for 'man'

Bomburra: Australian aborigine word for 'sleep'.

Colleen: Irish name for a girl.

Cove: A term for 'man'. Criminals in London developed their own 'flash' language, so that the general population would be none the wiser to their meanings. It was begun in the early nineteenth century, in the East End of London. It is now sometimes known as Australian slang.

Gaol:	An older variant of the word, 'jail'.
Gidya spear:	Spear made from accacia wood.
Gin:	A derogatory name for an aboriginal woman. Originating from the Dharuk tribe's word 'diyin', meaning 'woman' or 'wife'.
Government man:	Convict.
Gwandalan:	Australian aborigine word meaning 'rest', or 'peace'.
Humpies:	Bark shelters or huts.
Lum:	Old Scottish term for chimney
Slops:	The clothing worn by indentured labourers.
Stoved:	To break or crush.
Strumpet:	Prostitute or promiscuous woman.
Tap the admiral:	When Admiral Horatio Nelson was killed at the battle of Trafalgar, his body was said to have been preserved in a rum barrel until his burial could take place back in England. However, some of the sailors were said to have pierced the barrel with a gimlet (a type of knife) and drunk the rum through a straw, so that by the time they arrived on English soil, the barrel was almost empty. They had 'tapped the admiral', hence the term. Apparently this

	did not occur in reality; it is little more than an entertaining story.
Widdershins:	Anti-clock wise. Considered unlucky, or causing disaster, since the direction is counter-clockwise to the movement of the sun.
Worimi:	Australian aboriginal tribe that encompasses the New South Wales region of Maitland (known once as 'Wallis Plains'). Their people extended from the Port Stephens region, to that of Forster Tuncurry in the south, and stretched north-east by north to Gloucester. Flying fox, snake, goanna and kangaroo were known to be part of their diet, as well as food from the sea.

www.ingramcontent.com/pod-product-compliance
Lightning Source LLC
Chambersburg PA
CBHW032031290426
44110CB00012B/757